Future

BABYLON

The Biblical Arguments for the Rebuilding of Babylon

DR. CHARLES DYER

DISPENSATIONAL

PUBLISHING HOUSE, INC.

All Scripture quotations, unless otherwise indicated,
are taken from the New American Standard Bible®,
Copyright © 1960, 1962, 1963, 1968, 1971, 1972, 1973, 1975, 1977, 1995
by The Lockman Foundation
Used by permission. (www.Lockman.org)

Scripture quotations marked (NIV) are taken from the Holy Bible,
New International Version®, NIV®. Copyright © 1973, 1978, 1984, 2011 by Biblica, Inc.™
Used by permission of Zondervan. All rights reserved worldwide. www.zondervan.com
The "NIV" and "New International Version" are trademarks registered in the United States
Patent and Trademark Office by Biblica, Inc.™

Scripture quotations marked KJV are taken from the King James Version of the Bible.

Printed in the United States of America

First Edition, First Printing, 2017

ISBN: 9781945774058

Dispensational Publishing House, Inc.
220 Paseo del Pueblo Norte
Taos, NM 87571

www.dispensationalpublishing.com

Ordering Information:
Quantity sales. Special discounts are available on quantity purchases by churches, associations,
and others. For details, contact the publisher at the address above.

Orders by U.S. trade bookstores and wholesalers. Please contact the publisher:
Tel: (855) 437-9448

2 3 4 5 6 7 8 9 10 1

*This book is gratefully dedicated to Dr. Bill Bjork
and to the staff and congregation of
Grace Bible Church in Sun City, Arizona.
It is truly a blessing to serve the Lord with this
very special group of "senior saints"!*

Behold, how good and how pleasant it is
For brothers to dwell together in unity! (Ps. 133:1)

Table of Contents

Study Guide

Foreword

Charles Dyer is uniquely qualified to write a book about Babylon and Bible prophecy. Dyer wrote his master of theology thesis at Dallas Theological Seminary in the late 1970s on Babylon in Bible prophecy—more than a decade before any of the interest was stirred up by Saddam Hussein's invasion of Kuwait in 1990.

Dyer came to his conclusions about Babylon simply from an inductive study of the Bible years before the newspaper headlines blew up with the first Gulf War. What did blow up in August of 1990 was a desire to know what the Bible taught about Babylon in light of that war.

I went and made a taped interview of Dyer since he had gone in the late 1980s on two occasions to the Babylon Festival sponsored by Saddam Hussein and the Iraqi government. It was amazing to hear about how they were rebuilding that ancient city and honoring the great legacy of past Babylonian Empires.

I cannot think of a more informed person in all of evangelical Christianity who is more studied on the subject of Babylon, both Biblically and in terms of the contemporary issues, than Charles Dyer. I therefore highly recommend this new work on Babylon from his pen. Anyone, whether scholar or layman, will greatly profit from this book.

Dr. Thomas Ice
Executive Director
The Pre-Trib Research Center
August 2016

Acknowledgment

I want to thank Dr. Randy White and Paul Scharf for their encouragement and assistance in preparing this book for publication. Randy's passionate vision for Dispensational Publishing House and Paul's careful editorial oversight combined to make this a most enjoyable partnership!

"I thank my God in all my remembrance of you" (Phil. 1:3).

Introduction

Why examine the Biblical argument for the rebuilding of Babylon? It is this author's opinion that the hermeneutical issues surrounding Babylon are the very issues that affect dispensationalism and pretribulationalism. The approach one uses to interpret Biblical prophecy lies at the heart of both topics.

For most of Scripture, conservative evangelicals argue for historical, grammatical, literal interpretation.[1] However, when they come to *prophetic* passages many change their hermeneutical approach.[2] Dispensationalists and pretribulationists have argued that the best approach is to begin with the Old Testament passage itself and to determine the meaning of the

---

1 Thus Berkhof devotes one chapter to grammatical interpretation and a second chapter to historical interpretation (Louis Berkhof, *Principles of Biblical Interpretation* [Grand Rapids: Baker Book House, 1950], pp. 67-132). Mickelsen discusses "context," "language" and "history and culture" in his section on general hermeneutics (A. Berkeley Mickelsen, *Interpreting the Bible* [Grand Rapids: Wm. B. Eerdmans Publishing Co., 1963], pp. 99-177).

2 So Mickelsen describes three possible approaches: (a) "literal fulfillment of all details," (b) "the symbolic meaning of an entire prophecy," and (c) "equivalents, analogy, or correspondence" (Mickelson, *Interpreting the Bible*, pp. 296-98). He opts for the third method because a literal interpretation of passages such as Ezekiel 40–48 "should be abhorrent to everyone who takes seriously the message of the book of Hebrews" (Ibid., p. 298).

passage in its original historical context. Is the passage pointing toward the future? If so, to what is it pointing? It is the consistent use of the literal, historical method of interpretation that has resulted in dispensationalists distinguishing between Israel and the church and accepting a pretribulational rapture of the church before God resumes His program with Israel (cf. Dan. 9:27).

Though dispensationalists believe in literal interpretation, no one wants to be accused of being a *wooden literalist*. Literal interpretation allows for figures of speech and symbolic language, and all who claim to interpret literally still interpret some passages, images or events symbolically.[3] Still, one person's *symbol* is another person's literal prediction. And it is the differences in interpreting specific symbols that often determine one's position on eschatological events such as a pretribulational rapture.

The purpose of this volume is to examine the Biblical prophecies relating to the rebuilding of Babylon. However, a larger goal of this study is to explore the issue of literal interpretation as it relates to Babylon. The book will attempt to ask and answer three questions on the prophecies concerning Babylon.

THREE QUESTIONS ON THE PROPHECIES CONCERNING BABYLON	
FIRST	Why do Protestants interpret Babylon spiritually?
SECOND	What happened to Babylon historically?
THIRD	What does the Bible say about Babylon?

---

3 "The literal interpretation of Scripture readily admits the very large place which figurative language has in the Scriptures. . . . Literal interpretation does not mean painful, or wooden, or unbending literal rendition of every word and phrase" (Bernard Ramm, *Protestant Biblical Interpretation*, revised ed. [Boston: W. A. Wilde Co., 1956], p. 141).

CHAPTER 1

Why Do Protestants Interpret Babylon Spiritually?

The Influence of Luther and Calvin

The Reformation marked a turning point in interpreting Scripture. Luther and Calvin broke with the allegorical method that had dominated the church since Jerome and Augustine[4] and began interpreting Scripture in its grammatical/historical context. That is not to say that these early reformers were able to make a clean break with the allegorical method of interpretation. However, they did champion the

---

4 "It becomes clear from these late church fathers that Jerome, Vincent, and Augustine paved the way for two emphases that were to endure for more than a thousand years—allegorization and church authority" (Roy B. Zuck, *Basic Bible Interpretation* [Wheaton, IL: Victor Books, 1991], p. 41). Ramm says, "The allegorical system that arose among the pagan Greeks, copied by the Alexandrian Jews, was next adopted by the Christian church and largely dominated exegesis until the Reformation. . . ." (Ramm, *Protestant Biblical Interpretation*, p. 28).

grammatical/historical method for forming doctrine. Luther summarized his distinction between using the allegorical method for illustration and using the grammatical/historical method for interpretation:

> Let us forewarn here concerning allegory that it may be handled wisely in the Spirit. For playing games with the Sacred Scriptures has the most injurious consequences if the text and its grammar are neglected. From history we must learn well and much, but little from allegory. You use allegory as embellishment by which the discourse is illustrated but not established. Let history remain honest. It teaches, which allegory does not do. But this is what it means to teach: to instruct the conscience about what and how it should know, to nourish faith and the fear of God. In history you have the fulfillment of either promises or threats. Allegory does not pertain to doctrine, but to doctrine already established it can be added as color. The painter's color does not build the house. . . . Even so faith is not established by means of allegories.[5]

Luther's dedication to the historical meaning of the text resulted in his understanding of the doctrine of justification by faith. However, Luther was also a product of his times. In the midst of his struggles with Rome he was convinced that his present conflict had been predicted by the prophets.

> The appearance of the church under the papacy was exceedingly wretched. It has now revived again, and I am of the opinion that the last three woes in the Apocalypse have now passed and better times are beginning. I know for sure that this age, in which we now are, is better than the age in which the Jews were living at the time of Christ. However, the saying of Christ, "Then there will be great tribulation, such as has not been from the beginning" [Matt. 24:21], I understand to apply to the tribulation of the godly and not to the tribulation of the world when the pope persecuted the church. "If those days had not been shortened," the passage continues, "no human being would be saved" [Matt. 24:22]. This means that if our Lord God hadn't intervened through the gospel, the pope would have destroyed everything, and the gospel and the sacraments would have been lost together with the Holy Scriptures. Although there were great scandals among the Jews, under the papacy it was worse. For in former times only one people was thrown

---

5 Jaroslav Pelikan, ed. *Luther's Works*, Vol. 16, *Lectures on Isaiah 1–39* (Saint Louis: Concordia Publishing House, 1969), pp. 136-37.

into confusion, but under the papacy the whole world was unsettled. "He takes his seat in the temple of God" [II Thess. 2:4]. However, as I have said, the church is better off now than it was then.[6]

Luther's willingness to employ an allegorical or spiritual interpretation coupled with his belief that the prophecies of the end times were unfolding in his day led him to find specific references to the pope and the Roman Catholic Church—in the Antichrist and Babylon!

> But we, because we flee from and avoid all such deviltry and novelty and hold fast once more to the ancient church, the virgin and pure bride of Christ—we are certainly the true and ancient church, without any whoredom or innovation. This [Roman] church has therefore, remained till now, and it is out of it that we have come. Indeed, we have been born anew of it as the Galatians were of St. Paul [Gal. 4:19]. We too were formerly stuck in the behind of this hellish whore, this new church of the pope. We supported it in all earnestness, so that we regret having spent so much time and energy in that vile hole. But God be praised and thanked that he rescued us from the scarlet whore [Revelation 17].[7]

> No man can believe what an abomination the papacy is. A Christian does not have to be of low intelligence, either, to recognize it. God himself must deride him in the hellish fire, and our Lord Jesus Christ, St. Paul says in II Thessalonians 2 [:8], "will slay him with the breath of his mouth and destroy him by his glorious coming." I only deride, with my weak derision, so that those who now live and those who will come after us should know what I have thought of the pope, the damned Antichrist, and so that whoever wishes to be a Christian may be warned against such an abomination.[8]

Calvin, born 26 years after Luther, carried the Reformation in new directions with the publication of his *Institutes of the Christian Religion* in 1536. Calvin adopted Luther's view that the pope was the Antichrist and the Roman Catholic Church was Babylon.

---

6   Theodore G. Tappert, ed., *Luther's Works*, Vol. 54, *Table Talk*, "Beware of Melancholy and Trust God," No. 461, February 19, 1533 (Philadelphia: Fortress Press, 1967), pp. 76-77.

7   Eric W. Gritsch, ed., *Luther's Works*, Vol. 41, *Church and Ministry III*, "Against Hanswurst" (Philadelphia: Fortress Press, 1966), pp. 206-7.

8   Ibid., "Against the Roman Papacy, An Institution of the Devil," pp. 273-74.

Therefore, while we are unwilling simply to concede the name of the Church to the Papists, we do not deny that there are churches among them. The question we raise only related to the true and legitimate constitution of the Church, implying communion in sacred rites, which are the signs of profession, and especially in doctrine. Daniel and Paul foretold that Antichrist would sit in the temple of God (Dan. ix. 27; 2 Thess. ii. 4); we regard the Roman Pontiff as the leader and standard-bearer of that wicked and abominable kingdom. By placing his seat in the temple of God, it is intimated that his kingdom would not be such as to destroy the name either of Christ or his Church. Hence, then, it is obvious that we do not at all deny that churches remain under this tyranny; churches, however, which by sacrilegious impiety he has profaned, by cruel domination has oppressed, by evil and deadly doctrines like poisoned potions has corrupted and almost slain; churches where Christ lies half-buried, the gospel is suppressed, piety is put to flight, and the worship of God almost abolished; where, in short, all things are in such disorder as to present the appearance of Babylon rather than the holy city of God.[9]

The Historical Assumptions about Babylon's Fall

While Luther and Calvin saw a prophetic application of Babylon to Rome, both based their identification primarily on the Babylonian harlot of Revelation 17. As near as can be determined, both Luther and Calvin assumed the Old Testament prophecies of Babylon's fall were fulfilled historically when Babylon fell to Cyrus in 539 B.C. Luther identified the army being mustered together for war against Babylon in Isaiah 13:4 as "the soldiery and armed host of the Persians and Medes."[10] When Isaiah predicted that the Jews would return to the land after Babylon's fall (Isa. 14:1-4), Luther says, "All these things were done under Cyrus, king of the Persians, who permitted the Jews conquered by the Babylonians to return to their own land."[11]

---

9 John Calvin, *Institutes of the Christian Religion*, trans. Henry Beveridge (Grand Rapids: Wm. B. Eerdmans Publishing Co., 1962), 2:313-14.

10 Luther, *Isaiah 1–39*, p. 133.

11 Ibid., p. 138.

Most Protestant interpreters since Luther and Calvin have followed them in assuming that the Old Testament prophecies of Babylon were fulfilled historically. McDowell listed a series of eight specific prophecies on the destruction of Babylon from the Old Testament, and he concludes by stating categorically, "All eight predictions have been fulfilled."[12] Even critical scholars associate the various Old Testament prophecies with the fall of Babylon to Cyrus.[13] Certainly the consensus of opinion is that the Old Testament prophecies were fulfilled historically when Babylon fell to Cyrus.

---

12 Josh McDowell, comp. *Evidence That Demands a Verdict: Historical Evidences for the Christian Faith* (Arrowhead Springs, CA: Campus Crusade for Christ International, 1972), p. 319. The specific prophecies are: (a) "Babylon to be like Sodom and Gomorrah," (b) "Never inhabited again," (c) "Tents will not be placed there by Arabs," (d) "Sheepfolds will not be there," (e) "Desert creatures will infest the ruins," (f) "Stones will not be removed for other construction projects," (g) "The ancient city will not be frequently visited," and (h) "Covered with swamps of water" (Ibid., p. 315).

13 One example among many is Otto Kaiser, who dates Isaiah 13 to the postexilic period because of its description of Babylon's fall to Cyrus. "An older, late pre-exilic or more probably exilic prophecy may lie behind 13:2-22. In its present form it is post-exilic, and its outlook allows us to describe it as proto-apocalyptic. The taunt on the fall of the tyrant in 14:b-21 is also likely to be a product of the post-exilic period. Interest in the fate of Babylon did not come to an end with the conquest of the city by Cyrus in the year 539" (Otto Kaiser, *Isaiah 13–39. A Commentary*, trans. by R. A. Wilson, The Old Testament Library [Philadelphia: Westminster Press, 1974], p. 2).

CHAPTER 2

What Happened to Babylon Historically?

B efore examining the specific Old and New Testament prophecies about Babylon, one must first know the history of this city. This second section will trace Babylon's history from the time of Isaiah through today. The goal of this section is to use all available historical sources to answer the question: What happened to Babylon historically?

Babylon's Temporary Destruction by Sennacherib (689 B.C.)

Beginning with Merodach-Baladan, Babylon and Assyria entered a period of conflict much like that experienced between Israel/Judah and Assyria. Sennacherib conducted several campaigns against Babylon to bring the rebellious city back under his control.[14] Following the final conflict with Mushzib-Marduk, Sennacherib ordered his troops to destroy Babylon. "I made its destruction more complete than that by a flood. That in days to come, the site of that city, and (its) temples and gods, might not be remembered, I completely blotted it out with (floods) of water and made it like a meadow."[15] Babylon remained in ruins throughout the remainder of Sennacherib's reign (the next eight years, 689–681 B.C.). The Babylonian Chronicle notes this period by simply recording, "Eight years there was no king in Babylon."[16]

Sennacherib's son, Esarhaddon, was in charge of administering the region of Babylon while he was crown prince. After becoming king in 681 he began rebuilding Babylon and restoring the ancient temples.[17] The work was not completed until 669—the year Esarhaddon died.

Babylon's Fall to Cyrus (539 B.C.)

The Neo-Babylonian Empire can be traced to Nabopolassar, who seized the throne of Babylon in 626 B.C. He led the attack that destroyed the city of Nineveh in 612 B.C., and he ruled until 605 B.C. His son, Nebuchadnezzar, is the king who brought the Neo-Babylonian empire to its zenith of power. Nebuchadnezzar reigned from 605 to 562 B.C., and he was responsible for destroying the kingdom of Judah and for beginning "the times of the Gentiles" (Luke 21:24; cf. Dan. 2).

Following Nebuchadnezzar's death, the Neo-Babylonian empire began its decline. The next 23 years saw four kings ascend the throne (not

---

14   In fact, Babylon was first on Sennacherib's list of rebellious cities to attack. "In my first campaign I accomplished the defeat of Merodach-baladan, king of Babylonia. . . ." (Daniel David Luckenbill, *The Annals of Sennacherib*, 2 vols. [Chicago: University of Chicago Press, 1924], 2:24).

15   Ibid., 2:84.

16   Ibid., 2:161.

17   *The International Standard Bible Encyclopedia*, 1979 ed., s.v., "Babylon," by D. J. Wiseman, 1:385.

including Belshazzar who reigned as coregent with his father). The end of the Neo-Babylonian empire came at the hands of Cyrus in 539 B.C. The Babylonian Chronicle provides a concise account of Babylon's fall:

> In the month Tishri when Cyrus (II) did battle of Opis on the [bank of] the Tigris against the army of Akkad, the people of Akkad retreated. He carried off the plunder (and) slaughtered the people. On the four-teenth day [i.e., October 10, 539 B.C.] Sippar was captured without a battle. Nabonidus fled. On the sixteenth day [i.e., October 12, 539 B.C.] Ugbaru, governor of the Guti, and the army of Cyrus (II) entered Babylon without a battle. Afterwards, after Nabonidus retreated, he was captured in Babylon. Until the end of the month the shield-(bearing troops) of the Guti surrounded the gates of Esagil. (But) there was no interruption (of rites) in Esagil or the (other) temples and no date (for a performance) was missed. On the third day of the month Marchesvan [i.e., October 29, 539 B.C.] Cyrus (II) entered Babylon. . . . were filled before him. There was peace in the city while Cyrus (II) spoke (his) greeting to all of Babylon.[18]

The Babylonian Chronicle account is corroborated by an inscription found on a clay barrel. The inscription was an edict by Cyrus explaining why the gods had allowed him to capture Babylon. The inscription concludes by recording Cyrus' generous treatment of both the people of Babylon and the gods that had been held captive in Babylon.

> When I entered Babylon (DIN.TIRki) as a friend and (when) I established the seat of the government in the palace of the ruler under jubilation and rejoicing, Marduk, the great lord, [induced] the magnanimous inhabitants of Babylon (DIN.TIRki) [to love me], and I was daily endeavouring to wor-ship him. My numerous troops walked around in Babylon (DIN.TIRki) in peace, I did not allow anybody to terrorize (any place) of the [country of Sumer] and Akkad. I strove for peace in Babylon (Ká.dingir.raki) and in all his (other) sacred cities. As to the inhabitants of Babylon (DIN.TIRki), [who] against the will of the gods [had/were . . . , I abolished] the corvée (lit.: yoke) which was against their (social) standing. I brought relief to their dilapidated housing, putting (thus) an end to their (main) complaints.

---

18   A. K. Grayson, *Assyrian and Babylonian Chronicles* in *Texts from Cuneiform Sources*, ed. A. Leo Oppenheim (Locust Valley, NY: J. J. Augustin Publisher, 1975), pp. 109-10.

Marduk, the great lord, was well pleased with my deeds and sent friendly blessings to myself, Cyrus, the king who worships him, to Cambyses, my son, the offspring of [my] loins, as well as to all my troops, and we all [praised] his great [godhead] joyously, standing before him in peace.

All the kings of the entire world from the Upper to the Lower Sea, those who are seated in throne rooms, (those who) live in other [types of buildings as well as] all the kings of the West land living in tents, brought their heavy tributes and kissed my feet in Babylon. (As to the region) from . . . as far as Ashur and Susa, Agade, Eshnunna, the towns Zamban, Me-Turnu, Der as well as the region of the Gutians, I returned to (these) sacred cities on the other side of the Tigris, the sanctuaries of which have been ruins for a long time, the images which (used) to live therein and established for them permanent sanctuaries. I (also) gathered all their (former) inhabitants and returned (to them) their habitations. Furthermore, I resettled upon the command of Marduk, the great lord, all the gods of Sumer and Akkad whom Nabonidus has brought into Babylon to the anger of the lord of the gods, unharmed, in their (former) chapels, the places which make them happy.

May all the gods whom I have resettled in their sacred cities ask daily Bel and Nebo for a long life for me and may they recommend me (to him); to Marduk, my lord, they may say this: "Cyrus, the king who worships you, and Cambyses, his son, . . ." . . . all of them I settled in a peaceful place . . . ducks and doves, . . . I endeavoured to fortify/repair their dwelling places. . . .[19]

Babylon's Later History (530 B.C.–A.D. 1975)

Babylon's later history can be traced through the Medo-Persian and Greek periods by focusing on several key historical points. Cyrus was followed to the throne by Cambyses (530–522), Pseudo-Smerdis (522) and Darius I (522–486). At the time of Cambyses's death two revolts took place in Babylon. According to Herodotus, when Darius was finally able to put down these revolts he tried to weaken Babylon to prevent further

---

19 James B. Pritchard, *Ancient Near Eastern Texts Relating to the Old Testament*, 3d ed. (Princeton, NJ: Princeton University Press, 1969), p. 316.

insurrection. "Having mastered the Babylonians, Darius destroyed their walls and reft away all their gates, neither of which things Cyrus had done at the first taking of Babylon; moreover he impaled about three thousand men that were chief among them; as for the rest, he gave them back their city to dwell in."[20]

There is some question as to whether Darius destroyed all the walls of the city or only the gates and, perhaps, portions of the outer wall on the eastern side. Herodotus visited Babylon about 450 B.C., approximately 70 years after Darius' attack. From his eyewitness description it appears that the gates of the city were no longer in place, but most (if not all) of the walls were still standing. "Further, at the end of each road there *was* a gate in the riverside fence, one gate for each alley; these gates also *were* of bronze, and these too opened on the river. These [outer] walls *are* the city's outer armour; within them there *is* another encircling wall, well nigh as strong as the other, but narrower."[21] Herodotus also reports that the royal palace was still standing along with the temple complex of Marduk (which he calls Zeus Belus) and the tower of Babel.[22]

Herodotus' eyewitness account also calls into question later accounts of Babylon's destruction at the hands of Xerxes (485–465 B.C.). Arrian records that "the temple of Belus was in the midst of the city of Babylon, in size immense, and made of baked brick with bitumen for mortar. This temple, like the other shrines of Babylon, Xerxes razed to the ground, when he returned from Greece . . . ."[23] Perhaps the accounts can be harmonized by

---

20 Herodotus, 3.159.

21 Ibid., 1.180-81. Italics added to emphasize verb tenses.

22 Ibid., p. 181. "In the midmost of one division stands the royal palace, surrounded by a high and strong wall; and in the midmost of the other is still to this day the sacred enclosure of Zeus Belus, a square of two furlongs each way, with gates of bronze. In the centre of this enclosure a solid tower has been built, of one furlong's length and breadth; a second tower rises from this, and from it yet another, till at last there are eight."

23 Arrian, *Anabasis of Alexander*, 7.17.1. Strabo (63 B.C.–A.D. 24) seems to agree with Arrian when he writes, "Here too is the tomb of Belus, now in ruins, having been demolished by Xerxes, as it is said. It was a quadrangular pyramid of baked brick, not only being a stadium in height, but also having sides a stadium in length" (Strabo, *Geography*, 16.1.5). However, Strabo's account is

assuming that Xerxes damaged or ransacked the temple of Marduk proper without destroying the entire complex or the tower structure. In any case, the walls of Babylon, the temple complex of Marduk, and the tower of Babel were still in existence *after* the time of Xerxes when Herodotus visited the site, though they may have been in some state of disrepair.

Babylon also played a significant role in the life of Alexander the Great. Having conquered the world, Alexander returned to Babylon. He was busy making the city his chief city in the eastern part of his empire when he died. According to Strabo, Alexander began repairing and rebuilding the tower of Babel. "Alexander intended to repair this pyramid; but it would have been a large task and would have required a long time (for merely the clearing away of the mound was a task for ten thousand men for two months), so that he could not finish what he had attempted. . . ."[24] When Alexander's general, Hephaestion, died, Alexander "ordered a pyre to be made ready for him in Babylon at a cost of ten thousand talents. . . ."[25] In his excavations in Babylon, Robert Koldewey uncovered a series of mounds which the local population referred to as "Humaira." The archaeological discoveries in this area support the accounts of Arrian and Strabo and tie both together.

> The central mound consists of debris of broken bricks, among which an artificial platform was found, marked by traces of a great conflagration. These ruins are believed to mark the site of the funeral pyre erected by order of Alexander for the funeral of Hephaestion. The northernmost mound, c. 16 m high, consists of nothing but brick rubble, artificially heaped up. Some of the brick fragments bear Nebuchadnezzar's name and record the building of Etemenanki. Indeed it would seem that this is the actual debris removed by Alexander when he decided to rebuilt [*sic*] the ziggurat, which was in ruins when he reached Babylon.[26]

---

both late and unreliable. He confuses the temple of Marduk with the tower of Babel. Based on his knowledge of Egypt he assumes that the tower structure marked a tomb (as did the Egyptian pyramids).

24 Strabo, *Geography*, 16.1.5.

25 Arrian, *Anabasis of Alexander*, 7.14.8.

26 Joan Oates, *Babylon*, revised ed. (New York: Thames and Hudson, 1986), pp. 159-60.

Alexander's plan was to establish Babylon as his chief city in the east. "Alexander dug a harbour at Babylon, large enough to be a roadstead for a thousand ships of war, and dockyards on the harbour."[27] A Greek theater was also constructed in Babylon that could seat 4,000. It is unclear who built the theater. But its location in Humaira near the funeral pyre and the debris from Etemenanki point to the time of Alexander for its construction.[28] But Alexander's plans for Babylon were cut short when he died in Babylon at the age of 32.

After the division of Alexander's empire among his generals, Babylon was seized by Seleucus in 312 B.C. Seleucus later founded the city of Seleucia further north on the Tigris River, and this city replaced Babylon as the capital city of the empire. Yet Babylon remained an important religious and political center. Both Seleucus and his son, Antiochus I, retained the title "king of Babylon."[29]

The Parthians pushed into Mesopotamia between 166 and 122 B.C. and eventually established their capital at Ctesiphon.[30] During the Parthian era, Ctesiphon became the civil center, Seleucia remained the commercial center, while Babylon continued as the religious center. Josephus records that a large number of Jews were still living in Babylon during the Parthian period. "When Hyrcanus was brought into Parthia, the king of Phraates treated him after a very gentle manner, as having already learned of what

---

27 Arrian, *Anabasis of Alexander,* 7.19.4.

28 So Oates writes, "The Greek theatre in Babylon was first built at or not long after the time of Alexander and was reconstructed under his Seleucid successors" (Oates, *Babylon,* p. 143).

29 Pritchard, *Ancient Near Eastern Texts,* p. 317. An inscription from the time of Antiochus I reads in part, "I am Antiochus (*An-ti-'u-ku-us*), the great king, the legitimate king, the king of the world, king of Babylon (eki), king of all countries, the caretaker of the temples of Esagila and Ezida, the first(-born) son of king Seleucus (*Si-lu-uk-ku*), the Macedonian (*amelMa-ak-ka-du-na-a-a*), king of Babylon."

30 So Strabo writes, "Now in ancient times Babylon was the metropolis; but Seleuceia is the metropolis now, I mean the Seleuceia on the Tigris as it is called. Near by is situated a village called Ctesiphon, a large village. This village the kings of the Parthians were wont to make their winter residence, thus sparing the Seleuceians, in order that the Seleuceians might not be oppressed by having the Scythian folk or soldiery quartered amongst them. Because of Parthian power, therefore, Ctesiphon is a city rather than a village. . . ." (Strabo, *Geography,* 16.1.16).

an illustrious family he was; on which account he set him free from his bonds, and gave him a habitation at Babylon, where there were Jews in great numbers."[31]

Whitson believes Josephus is mistaken in his identification of Babylon as the site where Hyrcanus was settled. "The city here called 'Babylon' by Josephus seems to be one which was built by some of the Seleucidæ, upon the Tigris; which, long after the utter desolation of Old Babylon was commonly so called, just as the later adjoining city Bagdat [sic] is often called by the same old name of Babylon."[32]

If Whitson is correct, then Josephus' reference to Babylon has no merit because Josephus would have confused Babylon with either Seleucia or Ctesiphon. However, Josephus seems to know the difference between all three cities. Later in his account he records an incident where "a pestilence came upon these [Jews] at Babylon, which occasioned new removals of men's habitations out of that city; and because they came to Seleucia, it happened that a still heavier calamity came upon them."[33] Josephus had earlier demonstrated his familiarity with Seleucia by describing it as "the principal city of those parts, which was built by Seleucus Nicator. . . ."[34] After describing the massacre of 50,000 Jews who had fled from Babylon to Seleucia, Josephus reports that those who managed to escape "retired to Ctesiphon, a Grecian city, and situated near to Seleucia, where the king [of Parthia] lives in winter every year. . . ."[35] The point here is that Josephus clearly distinguishes between the three cities of Babylon, Seleucia and Ctesiphon. When Josephus refers to Jews living in Babylon, one should assume that Josephus knew which city he had in mind.

Strabo (63 B.C.–A.D. 24) reported that Babylon, while still in existence

---

31 Josephus, *Antiquities of the Jews*, 15.2.2.
32 William Whitson, trans. *Josephus. Complete Works* (Grand Rapids: Kregel Publications, 1978), p. 315.
33 Josephus, *Antiquities*, 18.9.8.
34 Ibid.
35 Ibid., 18.9.9.

in his day, was in decline. "What is more, Seleuceia at the present time has become larger than Babylon, whereas the greater part of Babylon is so deserted that one would not hesitate to say what one of the comic poets said in reference to the Megalopolitans in Arcadia: 'The Great City is a great desert.'"[36] And yet one cannot read too much into Strabo's words because he goes on to describe the buildings and homes constructed there. He also mentions the religious groups still living in Babylon. "In Babylonia a settlement is set apart for the local philosophers, the Chaldaeans, as they are called, who are concerned mostly with astronomy. . . ."[37]

Pliny (A.D. 23–79) gives a similar report on the condition of Babylon in his day. The city had lost most of its former glory, but it still maintained its religious significance. "The temple of Jupiter Belus in Babylon is still standing—Belus was the discoverer of the science of astronomy; but in all other respects the place has gone back to a desert, having been drained of its population by the proximity of Seleucia. . . ."[38]

While one cannot be dogmatic, it seems likely that a Jewish community continued to exist in Babylon during the first century A.D. On the day of Pentecost, Jews "of Mesopotamia" gathered with others from the diaspora in Jerusalem (Acts 2:9). Some of those other Jews who gathered came from "Cappadocia, Pontus and Asia, Phrygia and Pamphylia" (Acts 2:9-10). Jewish believers from these areas are included with Gentiles as the recipients of Peter's first epistle which he wrote: "To those who reside as aliens, scattered throughout Pontus, Galatia, Cappadocia, Asia, and Bithynia" (1 Pet. 1:1). Having written to these believers among the diaspora, Peter, the apostle to the Jews (cf. Gal. 2:8-10), closes his epistle by extending a greeting from "She [i.e., the church] who is in Babylon" (1 Pet. 5:13). While some see this as a coded reference to Rome,[39] it

---

36 Strabo, *Geography*, 16.1.5.
37 Ibid., 16.1.6.
38 Pliny, *Natural History*, 6.30.121-22.
39 So Selwyn writes that Babylon is "a *soubriquet* for Rome. . . . The objection to the Mesopotamian

hardly seems necessary for Peter to use such coded language. It seems more likely that Peter, while visiting one enclave of Jewish believers in Babylon, wrote a letter to another enclave of Jewish and Gentile believers in Asia Minor.[40]

With the close of the New Testament the information on Babylon becomes very sparse. Writers quote Dio who says Trajan visited Babylon in A.D. 116 and found "nothing but mounds and stones and ruins. . . ."[41] However, Dio's account should not be accepted uncritically. First, he also says Trajan offered sacrifices to Alexander "in the room where he had died."[42] If true, this implies that (a) some buildings were still standing and (b) someone still lived in Babylon who could point out the room to Trajan. Second, Dio also records Trajan's visit to the pit where the bitumen was mined for Babylon. He describes the pit as a place where deadly vapors "destroy any terrestrial animal and any winged creature" who might venture in except "human beings that have been emasculated. The reason for this I cannot understand."[43] He seems subject to exaggeration.

The next western source that can be clearly identified in Babylon is the Jewish traveler from Spain, Benjamin of Tudela, who visited the site 1,000 years after Trajan. He left a fascinating account of his travels to the Middle East, including a visit to Baghdad, Babylon and Hilla.

> From thence [i.e., Ras-al-Ain which was two days from Baghdad] it is one day to Babylon. This is the ancient Babel, and now lies in ruins; but the streets still extend thirty miles. The ruins of the palace

---

Babylon being intended is that there is no local tradition of any Apostle other than St. Thomas being associated with those parts. . . . In the case of I Peter, reasons of prudence may have dictated the use of the symbolic name, as the letter might have to pass the censorship of police officers" (Edward Gordon Selwyn, *The First Epistle of St. Peter* [New York: Macmillan & Co., 1964], p. 243).

40 Wuest cites six reasons for understanding Babylon in its literal sense. One reason is that "the other geographical references in First Peter have undoubtedly the literal meaning, and it would be natural to expect that Peter's use of the name 'Babylon' would be literal also" (Kenneth S. Wuest, *Wuest's Word Studies* [Grand Rapids: Wm. B. Eerdmans Publishing Co., 1966], 2:132-33).

41 Cassius Dio Cocceianus, *Dio's Roman History*, 68.30.

42 Ibid.

43 Ibid., 68.1-3.

of Nebuchadnezzar are still to be seen; but people are afraid to venture among them on account of the serpents and scorpions with which they are infested. Twenty thousand Jews live within about twenty miles from this place, and perform their worship in the synagogue of Daniel, who rests in peace. This synagogue is of remote antiquity, having been built by Daniel himself; it is constructed of solid stones and bricks. Here the traveller [*sic*] may also behold the palace of Nebuchadnezzar, with the burning fiery furnace into which were thrown Hananiah, Mishael, and Azariah; it is a valley well known to every one. Hillah, which is at a distance of five miles, contains about ten thousand Jews and four synagogues. . . .[44]

Benjamin of Tudela's description is a complex picture of a city largely in ruins but which still has some measure of habitation. He mentions that people are afraid to venture into Nebuchadnezzar's palace; but he then describes Daniel's synagogue, which is close to Nebuchadnezzar's palace in the city, and says it is visited by 20,000 Jews.

Benjamin of Tudela's description fits well with the descriptions of Pliny and other ancient writers. Much of the ancient city of Babylon was in ruins. However, the site was still inhabited and still held religious significance. But later western writers seem to paint a more desolate picture of Babylon. For example, in 1574 the German traveler Rauwolf traveled to Mesopotamia and wrote of his experiences. His description of the "ruins of Babylon" is more typical of the writings of later Europeans who describe Babylon as totally desolate and uninhabited.

> The village of Elugo, now lieth on the place where formerly old Babylon, the metropolis of Chaldæa, was situated. The harbour is a quarter of a league's distance from it, where people go ashore in order to proceed by land to the celebrated city of Bagdat, which is a day and a half's journey from thence eastward on the Tigris. . . . Just before the village of Elugo is the hill whereon the castle stood, and the ruins of its fortifications are still visible, though demolished and uninhabited. Behind it, and pretty near to it, did stand the tower of

---

44 "The Travels of Rabbi Benjamin of Tudela. A.D. 1160–1173," Thomas Wright, ed. *Early Travels in Palestine*, reprint ed. (New York: KTAV Publishing House, 1968), p. 100.

Babylon.—It is still to be seen, and is half a league in diameter; but so ruinous, so low, and so full of venomous creatures, which lodge in holes made by them in the rubbish, that no one durst approach nearer to it than within half a league, except during two months in the winter, when these animals never stir out of their holes. [45]

Rauwolf's description of Babylon's utter desolation, while vivid and dramatic, is also incorrect. The "village of Elugo" which he identified as ancient Babylon is known today as *Al Fallujah*. It is on the Euphrates River and was the spot where travelers left their boats to continue by land to Baghdad.[46] Unfortunately, the ancient site of Babylon is still 75 miles further south on the Euphrates River. Rauwolf never set eyes on the city of Babylon. In fact, many of the descriptions by many western visitors are not of Babylon but of other ruins in southern Mesopotamia that were within visiting distance of Baghdad.

Not much information can be found on Babylon during the remainder of the Middle Ages, but there is information that the city has been inhabited in the modern era, from at least the 1700s. Koldewey, the German archaeologist responsible for much of the work which has been done at Babylon, makes an interesting comment on the villages around the city. He described the site of the city and its ruins in this way:

At the bend of the Euphrates, between Babil and Kasr lie *the ruins of the former village of Kweiresh, whose population migrated elsewhere a hundred years ago.* The walls of mud brick still overtop the heaps of debris.

The modern village of Kweiresh lies close to the Kasr, to which we must now turn our attention. The most northerly house of Kweiresh is the headquarters of our expedition (Fig. 12), called by the Arabs "Kasr abid" [italics added].[47]

---

45 As cited by Thomas Newton, *Dissertations on the Prophecies* (London, J. F. Dove, n.d.), pp. 140-41.

46 Pilgrims and other travelers from the west would journey inland through what is today Syria until they reached the Euphrates River. They would float downriver to *Al Falljah* and then travel due east approximately 40 miles to Baghdad. For a map showing *Al Falljah* and describing its historic significance see *Lands of the Bible Today with Descriptive Notes* (Washington, D.C.: National Geographic Society, 1967).

47 Robert Koldewey, *The Excavations at Babylon*, trans. by Agnes S. Johns (London: Macmillan and Co., 1914), p. 22.

Koldewey makes two important statements. First, he states definitely that a village was existing in his day within the walls of the ancient city of Babylon. He headquartered in this village as he excavated the nearby ruins. Second, Koldewey reports the existence of another village (with the same name) that had also existed within the city of Babylon a century earlier. Since he gives only an approximate date of abandonment, there is no way to determine how long that earlier city had existed in Babylon; but the permanence of the structures would suggest an extended history. Koldewey presents a detailed map of Babylon's ruins in which he shows the location of both the ancient village of Kweiresh as well as the modern village. Both are in the heart of what was once ancient Babylon.[48]

Babylon Today

Koldewey has shown that Babylon was still inhabited at least at the time of his excavations in the early 1900s. However, what is the status of Babylon today? In 1978 Mrs. L. Glynne Dairos, assistant secretary of the British School of Archaeology in Iraq, responded to a question from this writer on the existence of any modern villages within the walls of the ancient city. She wrote, "There are three modern settlements situated inside the walls of ancient Babylon. The government of Iraq does indeed plan to restore much of Babylon and has indeed made a start on certain buildings."[49]

To understand what is happening in Babylon today one must first understand the political ambitions once held by Saddam Hussein. During the Iran/Iraq War, Hussein used the city of Babylon as a visual aid to remind the Iraqi people of the history of conflict between Iraq and Iran and of the territorial ambitions of the Iranians. As Paul Lewis wrote in

---

48   Ibid., fig. I.

49   L. Glynne Dairos, Assistant Secretary of the British School of Archaeology in Iraq, to Charles H. Dyer, Dallas, 15 August 1978. Personal files of Charles H. Dyer, Dallas, Texas.

the *New York Times International*, "President Hussein's decision to rebuild Nebuchadnezzar's Palace at the height of a war he almost lost was the centerpiece of a campaign to strengthen Iraqi nationalism by appealing to history. . . . Mr. Hussein's campaign also served subtler ends; it justified Iraq's costly war with Iran as the continuation of Mesopotamia's ancient feud with Persia. And it portrayed Saddam Hussein as successor to Nebuchadnezzar, Babylon's mightiest ruler."[50]

In effect, Saddam Hussein used Babylon as an Iraqi *Alamo* or *Masada*. His decision to rebuild Babylon forced the people to focus on a grand era in Iraq's history that was destroyed by the same enemy who again threatened the nation. It is no accident that the Babylon being rebuilt by Hussein was the Babylon of Nebuchadnezzar. As early as 1986, Michael Dobbs, writing in *The Washington Post*, noticed that the restoration of Babylon had become a political (not merely an archaeological) undertaking. "The Iraqis view Babylon somewhat differently [than the Bible]. For the Iraqi government, the Babylonian Empire is a source of national pride and inspiration for the grueling six-year-old war with neighboring Iran, Iraq's hereditary enemy. . . . President Saddam Hussein has ordered that no expense be spared to restore the city to its ancient splendor."[51]

Building Babylon became synonymous with rising to the threat of the Iranians and asserting Iraq's *manifest destiny* to lead the Arab nations to glory. Now, instead of just building Babylon as an archaeological park, Babylon became the focal point of Iraqi nationalism, which had replaced the earlier Baathist goal of Arab nationalism. By early 1987 plans were underway to hold the first annual Babylon Festival to celebrate the glory of Babylon, which included an emphasis on Saddam Hussein and Iraq. It is no accident that the opening of the festival was scheduled for September

---

50 *New York Times International*, April 19, 1989, p. 4-Y.
51 *Washington Post*, December 1, 1986, p. A-11.

22, 1987—seven years to the day after Iraq's invasion of Iran.[52]

While the Babylon Festival was announced as a cultural event featuring musical groups, symposia and other cultural activities, the festival had much deeper political overtones. This author attended the first Babylon Festival as an invited participant. One could not help but notice the emphasis placed on Saddam Hussein and the comparisons made between Saddam Hussein and Nebuchadnezzar. The official seal of the Babylon Festival featured the portraits of Saddam Hussein and Nebuchadnezzar side by side. The portraits were designed to stress physical similarities between the two men. The official theme of the Festival was "From Nabukhadnezzar [*sic*] to Saddam Hussein Babylon Undergoes a Renaissance."

On the opening night of the Babylon Festival Latif Nssayif Jassim, minister of information and culture, spoke to the audience that had gathered. His speech focused on the political and historical conflict between Iraq and Iran and the part played by Babylon in that conflict.

> However, the Persian [i.e., Iranian] mentality in our neighbourhood, prompted by deep-rooted hatred and aggressiveness tried to quench the flame of civilisation in this city of Babylon. Hence the city came under the attack of the Persian ruler Kurash (Cyrus) who, before 2,500 years, laid siege to this town. The siege lasted long and the town remained strong. It was not until Cyrus had collaborated with the Jews inside the city that he was able to tighten the siege round the city and subsequently to occupy it. . . . Today we are living in the midst of Khomeini's aggression which has extended over a span of seven years during which Khomeini had allied himself with the Zionists in an attempt to enter Baghdad and other Iraqi cities and to destroy them as was the case with Babylon. . . . It [i.e., rebuilt Babylon] will serve as a living example of the grandeur of the Iraqis to pursue their path for more glories.[53]

This writer's visits to Babylon in 1987 and 1988 confirm that much of the site was being rebuilt by Saddam Hussein. Hussein's agenda in

---

52 Starting the festival on the day that Iraq began the war by invading Iran was, as the *Baghdad Observer*, the official English-language newspaper in Iraq, observed, "not a mere coincidence" (*Baghdad Observer*, September 23, 1987, p. 1).

53 *Baghdad Observer*, September 23, 1987, p. 2.

rebuilding Babylon had nothing to do with Bible prophecy, but it had everything to do with his desire to promote his political agenda in the Middle East.

> Old policies have always ignored the status of Babylon when they created psychological and scientific barriers between Iraqis and their leaders in ancient times. No one has ever mentioned the achievements of "Hammurabi," the founder of the first organized set of law in human history. Or "Nebuchadnezzar," the national hero who was able to defeat the enemies of the nation on the land of "Kennan" [i.e., Canaan] and to take them as prisoner of war to Babylon. What we need now is to increase awareness in this regard.[54]

The third annual Babylon Festival was held in September 1989, but the fourth annual festival scheduled for September 1990 was canceled following Iraq's invasion of Kuwait. Operation Desert Shield and Operation Desert Storm became the dominant topic in that region of the world. When the smoke of battle cleared, many felt that Saddam Hussein's days were numbered. But amazingly he survived longer than the United States president who masterminded the coalition against Iraq.

But what about Babylon? The city was not damaged during the bombing in Operation Desert Storm. It was included on a list of sites off limits to bombing because of historical or archaeological importance. Work on the reconstruction of Babylon stopped following the invasion of Kuwait, but the reconstruction already completed remained intact. Within months after the end of Operation Desert Storm an article appeared in the *New York Times* describing the resumption of work at Babylon.

> One of President Hussein's favorite prestige projects has been the rebuilding of King Nebuchadnezzar's great southern palace in Babylon according to the designs of German archaeologists early this century. . . .
>
> Reconstruction has been more or less complete for a year now. And while archaeologists may bicker over details, this immense set of interconnecting

---

54 Quote attributed to Saddam Hussein in Babylon International Festival brochure for September 22, 1987.

chambers and courtyards surrounded by crenelated fortifications is more interesting for visitors than the pile of mud that used to be all there was to see at Babylon.

Today, however, the southern temple [*sic*, palace] is a desolate spot. Power and water have been cut off by the allied bombing, and its shops, museums and restaurants are closed. But work is under way on a series of three huge viewing platforms just outside the walls of Nebuchadnezzar's Babylon from which visitors will be able to look down at new excavations Iraq is planning.

"This is the personal orders of the President," said Iraq's Director General of Antiquities, Mouyad Said.[55]

On August 27, 1992, I received a fax from the Iraqi Interest Section of the Algerian Embassy. The fax read in part, "On the occasion of the Fourth Babylon Festival, the symposium of Babylon architecture will be held from September 1, 1992 to September 6, 1992 in Baghdad. We are pleased to invite you to participate in this symposium . . . ."[56] On June 28, 1993, another letter was received inviting me to "the Fifth Annual Babylon Festival to be held from September 22, 1993 to October 6, 1993."[57] The war may have slowed Saddam Hussein down, but it did not put an end to his plans to restore the city of Babylon.

---

55 Paul Lewis, "Dollars Can Still Get You Scotch and Waterford Crystal in Baghdad," *New York Times*, May 12, 1991, p. 10.

56 Personal correspondence from Dr. Mouayyad Said Damerji, Head of the Babylon Festival Organizing Committee, to Dr. Charles H. Dyer, 27 August 1992.

57 Personal correspondence from Khalid J. Shewayish, Chief of Iraq Interests Section at the Embassy of the Republic of Algeria, to Dr. Charles H. Dyer, 28 June 1993.

CHAPTER 3

What Does the Bible
Say about Babylon?

Having traced Babylon's history from the time of Isaiah until today, the focus must now turn to the Bible to place Babylon's history in prophetic perspective. Three Old Testament prophecies and one New Testament prophecy concerning Babylon will be briefly examined to determine what, if any, prophetic significance they might have.

Isaiah 13–14

In Isaiah 13–23 the prophet turns from Judah to deliver God's message to the surrounding Gentile nations. It is as if the prophet is telling these nations, "If God hasn't spared His own people, what makes you

Gentiles think you will escape?" This section is so large that it is often difficult to determine its structural significance. It often helps first to list the nations in order and to make any observations on the overall structure before examining the particular messages. The nations addressed by Isaiah are as follows:

NATIONS ADDRESSED BY ISAIAH		
NATION	**REFERENCE**	**TOTAL VERSES**
Babylon	13:1–14:23	45
Assyria	14:24-27	4
Philistia	14:28-32	5
Moab	15:1–16:14	23
Damascus and Samaria	17:1-14	14
Cush	18:1-7	7
Egypt	19:1-25	25
Egypt and Cush	20:1-6	6
Babylon	21:1-10	10
Edom	21:11-12	2
Arabia	21:13-17	5
Jerusalem	22:1-25	25
Tyre	23:1-18	18

Four principles of Bible study can help in evaluating this list of nations.

FIRST

The first principle is the principle of chiasm. If a list is structured as a chiasm, whatever is at the beginning and end of the chiasm, or whatever is in the center of the chiasm, might be that which the author is stressing. This principle does not apply to Isaiah 13–23 because the list is not structured as a chiasm.

SECOND

The second principle is the principle of perceived order in a list. Whatever the author places first or last in his list might be important. Isaiah placed Babylon first, and he placed Tyre last.

THIRD

The third principle is the law of proportion. In any list the author will spend more time on those items he intends to emphasize. If Cush and Egypt are counted as a unit, then the three nations on which Isaiah spends most of his time are Babylon (45 verses), Egypt and Cush (38 verses) and Jerusalem (25 verses).

FOURTH

The fourth principle is the principle of repetition. If an author repeats an item in his list, it could be important. In Isaiah 13–23 one nation is repeated twice— Babylon (13–14; 21).

This preliminary review of Isaiah 13–23 points out the importance of Babylon in Isaiah's messages against the nations. Isaiah begins his series of messages with Babylon, he spends more time on Babylon than on any other nation, and he has two separate messages against Babylon in the list. Thus Babylon must be important in the theme Isaiah is developing.

However, before continuing, one key issue must be explored. Some scholars have argued that the prophecies against Babylon in Isaiah 13 and 14 are actually focusing on Assyria and its king instead of Babylon. If this is true, then Isaiah's prophecies against Babylon might have no significance for the future of Babylon. But why do these scholars see Assyria rather than Babylon in Isaiah 13 and 14? Three basic reasons are given.

First, the structure of Isaiah 13–23 argues for identifying Assyria with Babylon. Each of Isaiah's messages against the nations is introduced with the word "oracle" ("the oracle concerning Babylon" [Isa. 13:1], etc.). But after describing the destruction of Babylon in 13:1–14:23, Isaiah does not use the word "oracle" to describe God's judgment against Assyria (14:24-27). "Many interpreters feel that these verses are a separate section. But it seems preferable to see them as part of the oracle beginning in 13:1."[58] Thus, the argument goes, Isaiah identifies the real subject of this oracle, Assyria, as he draws the oracle to a conclusion.

Second, identifying Babylon as Assyria would fit better historically in light of Assyria's dominant position on the international scene. "Many commentators have assumed that Isaiah's message in 13:1–14:27 about the fall of Babylon referred to its fall to Medo-Persia in 539. However, it seems better to see this section as pertaining to the Assyrian attack on Babylon in 689. This ties in better with the Assyrian threat Isaiah had written about in 7:17–8:10, beginning with the attacks under the rule of Tiglath-Pileser III (745–727)."[59] Assyria, not Babylon, was the nation threatening Judah in Isaiah's day, and it would make more sense for Isaiah to start his list of nations with Assyria.

Third, identifying Babylon as Assyria can be justified since the kings of Assyria took on the title "king of Babylon." "But wasn't Sennacherib king of Assyria rather than Babylon? He was king of both because Babylon was a vassal of Assyria from the end of the 10th century B.C. Occasionally the vassal ruler over Babylon revolted against Assyria, but in 728 Tiglath-Pileser III, Assyria's aggressive ruler from 745–727, was crowned king of Babylon. . . . Sargon II (722–705) and Sennacherib (705–681), later Assyrian monarchs, also called themselves kings of Babylon."[60] Thus, "the

58 John A. Martin, "Isaiah," in *The Bible Knowledge Commentary: Old Testament*, ed. by John F. Walvoord and Roy B. Zuck (Wheaton: Victor Books, 1985), p. 1,062.

59 Ibid., p. 1,058.

60 Ibid., p. 1,061.

king of Babylon" in Isaiah 14:4 would, in reality, have been the current king of Assyria.

THREE ARGUMENTS IN FAVOR OF AN ASSYRIAN IDENTIFICATION OF BABYLON IN ISAIAH 13–14

FIRST	The structure of Isaiah 13–23 argues for identifying Assyria with Babylon.
SECOND	Identifying Babylon as Assyria would fit better historically in light of Assyria's dominant position on the international scene.
THIRD	Identifying Babylon as Assyria can be justified since the kings of Assyria took on the title "king of Babylon."

How strong are the arguments for identifying Babylon as Assyria in Isaiah 13 and 14? Each of the arguments is not as strong as it might first appear.

ARGUMENTS AGAINST THE ASSYRIAN IDENTIFICATION OF BABYLON IN ISAIAH 13–14

FIRST	Isaiah's use of the term "oracle" cannot be used to associate Assyria with Babylon
SECOND	Second, assuming that Babylon must be equivalent to Assyria because Assyria was the dominant nation in Isaiah's day limits God's ability to speak to events that were still future.
THIRD	Claiming that the kings of Assyria took the title "king of Babylon" is not entirely correct.

First, Isaiah's use of the term "oracle" cannot be used to associate Assyria with Babylon. Isaiah does *not* consistently use "oracle" to separate each message against the nations. In 17:1 Isaiah introduces a new nation with his standard phrase: "The oracle concerning Damascus." Damascus and the Arameans lived northeast of Judah and were a constant source of trouble to the Israelites. However, in Isaiah 18:1 the prophet shifts to another nation—but he does not begin this new section with the word "oracle."

> Alas, oh land of whirring wings
> Which lies beyond the rivers of Cush,
> Which sends envoys by the sea,
> Even in papyrus vessels on the surface of the waters. (18:1-2a)

Cush was the land south of Egypt in the area today known as Sudan. There is no way Cush can be identified with Damascus, but Isaiah moved from one nation to the other without using "oracle" to introduce the break. Not using "oracle" between Babylon and Assyria in Isaiah 14:24 is no more unusual than not using "oracle" between Damascus and Cush in Isaiah 18:1. The absence of the word "oracle" does not demand that one link together Babylon and Assyria.

Second, assuming that Babylon must be equivalent to Assyria because Assyria was the dominant nation in Isaiah's day limits God's ability to speak to events that were still future. Such a position does not take into account the fact that Babylon was theologically significant from God's perspective (cf. Gen. 11:1-9). Nor does it account for Isaiah 39, where God predicts that Babylon would be the nation that would destroy the kingdom of Judah—a prophecy made while Assyria was still the dominant international power. God can predict more than current events, and Babylon is later identified as the nation that will destroy Judah.

Third, claiming that the kings of Assyria took the title "king of Babylon" is not entirely correct. While some at times did take this title, this does not seem to be the rule during much of the time Isaiah was prophesying.

In the Oriental Institute Prism Inscription (often called the Taylor Prism), Sennacherib gives a quite full listing of his titles: "Sennacherib, the great king, the mighty king, king of the universe, king of Assyria, king of the four quarters (of the earth); the wise ruler (lit. shepherd, 'pastor'), favorite of the great gods, guardian of the right, lover of justice; who lends support, who comes to the aid of the needy, who turns (his thoughts) to pious deeds; perfect hero, mighty man; first among all princes, the powerful one who consumes the insubmissive, who strikes the wicked with the thunderbolt. . . ."[61] His title in the Nebi Yunus inscription is very similar: "Palace of Sennacherib, the great king, the mighty king, king of the universe, king of Assyria, king of the four quarters (of the world); favorite of the great gods; wise sovereign, provident prince, shepherd of peoples, ruler of widespread nations, am I."[62] Of all the titles Sennacherib took in these inscriptions, "king of Babylon" was not one of them.

Both the Oriental Institute Prism and the Babylonian Chronicle support the contention that Sennacherib did not assume the title "king of Babylon" as a permanent title. In the Oriental Institute Prism, Sennacherib describes his defeat of "Merodach-Baladan, king of Babylon" in 703 b.c.[63] In 700 b.c. Sennacherib conducted a second campaign against Merodach-Baladan. Only after this defeat did Sennacherib replace Merodach-Baladan with another king. "I placed on his (Merodach-Baladan's) royal throne, Assur-nadin-shum, my oldest son, offspring of my loins (knees). I put him in charge of the wide land of Sumer and Akkad."[64] The Babylonian Chronicle provides a careful list of the kings of Babylon from Merodach-Baladan on, as well as the length of each one's rule. They included the following:

---

61 Luckenbill, *The Annals of Sennacherib*, 2:23.
62 Ibid., p. 85.
63 Ibid., p. 24.
64 Ibid., p. 35.

RULER	PERIOD	LENGTH OF THE RULE
Merodach-Baladan	721–710, 703 B.C.	13 years
Bel-ibni	702–700 B.C.	3 years
Assur-nadin-shum	699–694 B.C.	6 years
Nergal-ushezib	693 B.C.	1 1/2 years
Mushezib-Marduk	692–689 B.C.	4 years

Note: For 8 years there was no king (689–681 B.C.).[65]

Some kings of Assyria did claim the title "king of Babylon," but it was usually for a short period of time and was not automatically taken.

KINGS OF ASSYRIA WHO CLAIMED THE TITLE "KING OF BABYLON"	
Tiglath-pileser III	Claimed the title the final two years (729–727 B.C.) of his 19-year reign
Shalmaneser V	Claimed the title for most of his reign (726–722 B.C.)
Sargon II	Claimed the title in the later part of his reign (710–705 B.C.)
Sennacherib	May have claimed the title at the very beginning of his reign (704 B.C.)

---

65 Ibid., "Excerpts from the Babylonian Chronicle," pp. 158-61. For a concise listing of the rulers and their dates see Faraj Basmachi, *Treasures of the Iraq Museum* (Baghdad: Ministry of Information, Directorate General of Antiquities, 1976), p. 84.

Isaiah prophesied from 739 to 686 B.C. From 739 to 700 B.C. (the period when the prophecies against the nations were likely given), the Assyrians claimed the title "king of Babylon" for 14 years while for 26 years the title was held by someone other than the king of Assyria. From 703 B.C. to 681 B.C. (the time when Babylon's destruction occurred), Sennacherib did *not* claim the title "king of Babylon."

Otto Kaiser includes one final distinction between the prophecies against Babylon and Assyria that indicate the two are to be kept distinct. "But a further difference is immediately obvious: whereas Babylon is to be annihilated in its own country, the Assyrians are to fall in the Holy Land."[66] On the whole, it seems best to take Isaiah's words at face value and to identify the subject of his prophecy in 13:1–14:23 as Babylon.

But what does Isaiah say about Babylon in this initial prophecy? Isaiah provides three specific keys on the nature of the fulfillment one should expect for this prophecy. Each of these will be examined briefly.

THREE SPECIFIC KEYS ON THE NATURE OF THE FULFILLMENT OF ISAIAH 13:1–14:23

FIRST	The timing of the destruction.
SECOND	The nature of the destruction.
THIRD	The results of the destruction.

66 Kaiser, *Isaiah 13–23*, p. 2.

The timing of the destruction

Isaiah's first key focuses on the timing of Babylon's destruction. Having described the massing of the armies to attack (13:2-5), Isaiah announces:

> Wail, for the day of the LORD is near!
> It will come as destruction from the Almighty (Isa. 13:6).

While "the day of the LORD" could refer to any time in history when God intervenes in judgment (cf. Amos 5:18-20), Isaiah uses eschatological imagery that seems to go beyond a mere temporal judgment in his day. Otto Kaiser, who does not hold to Isaianic authorship, still recognizes the universal themes of judgment used by his so-called "proto-apocalyptic redactor." "Obviously the person responsible for the chapter as we have it was prepared to tolerate the tension which results from the interweaving of prophecies of a local and a universal future event."[67]

Isaiah defines "the day of the LORD" as a time of universal cataclysmic judgment. As he returns to the "day of the LORD" theme in 13:9, he describes it as:

> Cruel, with fury and burning anger,
> To make the land a desolation;
> And He will exterminate its sinners from it.

His description of supernatural signs in the heavens is very similar to that of Joel and, depending on when one dates the prophecies of Joel, could be borrowed from that prophet.

ISAIAH 13:9-10	JOEL 3:14–15
Behold, the day of the LORD is coming.... For the stars of heaven and their constellations Will not flash forth their light; The sun will be dark when it rises And the moon will not shed its light.	Multitudes, multitudes in the valley of decision! For the day of the LORD is near in the valley of decision. The sun and moon grow dark And the stars lose their brightness.

---

67 Ibid., p. 9.

In Isaiah 13 this judgment extends beyond just Babylon. The purpose for the day is to:

> Punish the world for its evil
> And the wicked for their iniquity. (13:11)

God's judgment on this day encompasses the world. After the judgment humanity will be "scarcer than pure gold" (13:12). Isaiah concludes his description on the time of judgment by stating it will be a time when God will disrupt both "the heavens ... and the earth" (13:13). While this could be a figure of speech, it also conjures up imagery of supernatural signs in the heavens and great earthquakes on earth that seem symbolic of the last days (cf. Zech. 14:3-7; Matt. 24:7, 29 [which quotes Isa. 13:10]; Rev. 6:12-14).

The nature of the destruction

Isaiah began with Babylon, but his imagery of the "day of the Lord" soared from "Babylon" (13:1), to "the whole land" (13:5), to "the world" (13:11), to "the heavens ... and the earth" (13:13). However, beginning in 13:14 Isaiah returns to describe the nature of the destruction about to be inflicted on Babylon. Babylon is to experience total annihilation.

> Anyone who is found will be thrust through,
> And anyone who is captured will fall by the sword.
> Their little ones also will be dashed to pieces
> Before their eyes;
> Their houses will be plundered
> And their wives ravished. (13:15-16)

Isaiah pictures a blood bath that will engulf warriors and women, soldiers and civilians.

In 13:17 Isaiah names one specific group participating in this attack: "Behold, I am going to stir up the Medes against them. . . ." Because Isaiah mentions the Medes, many interpreters have assumed the fulfillment of Isaiah's prophecy took place in 539 B.C., when Cyrus and the Medo-Persian empire captured Babylon. However, a careful comparison of Isaiah 13 with the events of 539 B.C. shows that this passage was *not* literally fulfilled at that time.

Isaiah describes "the Medes" as those, "Who will not value silver or take pleasure in gold" (13:17). Instead the purpose for the attack by the Medes will be to kill the inhabitants of Babylon.

> And *their* bows will mow down the young men,
> They will not even have compassion on the fruit of the womb,
> *Nor* will their eye pity children. (13:18)

While the Medes were part of the army that captured Babylon, they did not attack or kill the inhabitants of the city. Both the Babylonian Chronicle and Cyrus' own account record the peacefulness of Babylon's fall. Cyrus wrote, "My numerous troops walked around in Babylon (din. tirki) in peace, I did not allow anybody to terrorize (any place) of the [country of Sumer] and Akkad. I strove for peace in Babylon (Ká.dingir. raki) and in all his (other) sacred cities."[68] The Babylonian Chronicle adds, "Until the end of the month the shield-(bearing troops) of the Guti surrounded the gates of Esagil. (But) there was no interruption (of rites) in Esagil or the (other) temples and no date (for a performance) was missed. On the third day of the month Marchesvan [i.e., October 29, 539 B.C.] Cyrus (II) entered Babylon.... There was peace in the city while Cyrus (II) spoke (his) greeting to all of Babylon."[69] It seems inconsistent to say the prophecy was fulfilled in 539 by interpreting "Medes" literally while disregarding the fact that what is said about the Medes was *not* literally fulfilled.

---

68 Pritchard, *Ancient Near Eastern Texts Relating to the Old Testament*, p. 316.
69 Grayson, *Assyrian and Babylonian Chronicles* in *Texts from Cuneiform Sources*, pp. 109-10.

The results of the destruction

Isaiah focuses on two specific results of the attack against Babylon. First, he describes the permanence of Babylon's destruction. Babylon "will be as when God overthrew Sodom and Gomorrah" (13:19). By comparing Babylon's destruction to that of Sodom and Gomorrah, Isaiah conjures up a vivid image of total annihilation. Sodom and Gomorrah were suddenly, totally and permanently destroyed. Following their destruction they were never reinhabited.

Isaiah follows his pronouncement with three specific images that help define the extent of Babylon's destruction.

- Babylon will never again experience long-term habitation. "It will never be inhabited or lived in from generation to generation" (13:20a). Yet this could imply some type of semipermanent occupation, so Isaiah narrows the image still further.

- Babylon will never again experience even short-term habitation. "Nor will the Arab pitch *his* tent there" (13:20b). Nomadic settlers would often pitch their tents for months (sometimes even years) in one location before moving when supplies of water or grass for grazing became depleted. Babylon will not even experience the short-term occupation of nomadic settlers. But Isaiah adds a third illustration to reduce further the scope of habitation.

- Babylon will never again experience any human habitation. "Nor will shepherds make *their flocks* lie down there" (13:20c). Shepherds were constantly on the move to find enough grazing land for their flocks. As they led their flocks from their semipermanent dwelling places, they would often find themselves far from their tents at the end of the day. When darkness came, the shepherds would find a suitable spot for a sheepfold to bed their flock down for the night. At the break of dawn the shepherd and his flock would then move on.

Isaiah is saying that Babylon will not even serve as a dwelling place for an individual for a single evening.

Isaiah's imagery builds to a climax. Babylon's destruction will rival that of Sodom and Gomorrah. Once this destruction has come, Babylon will never again experience long-term habitation ("from generation to generation"). Babylon will not even experience temporary, short-term habitation ("tent[s]"). Babylon will not experience any habitation ("Nor will shepherds make *their flocks* lie down there"). Isaiah has used the most dramatic imagery available to announce to his readers that one result of Babylon's fall will be her sudden, complete and permanent destruction.

In Isaiah 14, the prophet describes a second result of Babylon's fall. In some way, Babylon's destruction will serve as a catalyst for God's restoration of His people.

> When the LORD will have compassion on Jacob and again choose Israel, and settle them in their own land, then strangers will join them and attach themselves to the house of Jacob. (14:1)

Babylon's fall is connected with God's restoration of His people to the land.

When Babylon fell to Cyrus in 539 B.C., Jews were allowed to return to the land of Judah. Could this return be what Isaiah had in mind? The remainder of Isaiah 14 implies that the answer is no. The return described by Isaiah is not merely a physical return of a remnant who would still remain under Gentile domination.

> The peoples will take them along and bring them to their place, and the house of Israel will possess them as an inheritance in the land of the LORD as male servants and female servants; and they will take their captors captive and will rule over their oppressors. (14:2)

Isaiah describes a return in which Israel becomes the dominant nation that will extend sovereign control over her former adversaries. One need only read Ezra, Nehemiah, Haggai or Zechariah to realize that this was not the situation following Babylon's fall to Cyrus in 539 B.C.

The prophecies of Isaiah 13 and 14 were not fulfilled literally in 539 B.C. Babylon did fall, the Medes were involved and a remnant from Israel did return to the land. However, Babylon continued to flourish as a city rather than being destroyed, the inhabitants of Babylon were not slaughtered, the day of the LORD did not extend to the world and Israel did not return to the land making captives of her former captors. Either Isaiah's prophecies were not intended to be taken literally or else this prophecy has not yet been fulfilled.

Jeremiah 50–51

A century after Isaiah penned his prophecy against Babylon, the city rose to become the center of power in the ancient Near East. Under Nebuchadnezzar, Babylon's influence extended from Persia to Egypt. In Judah, the young prophet Jeremiah predicted that Babylon would attack and destroy Jerusalem. Jeremiah's predictions came true in 586 B.C.

The book of Jeremiah is not in order chronologically. Instead, the book follows a thematic development.

> Take a scroll and write on it all the words which I have spoken to you concerning Israel and concerning Judah, and concerning all the nations.... (Jer. 36:2)

Chapters 2 to 45 focus on God's Word to Israel and Judah, while chapters 46 to 51 focus on God's Word to all the nations.

As in Isaiah, one should look at the overall structure of Jeremiah's messages against the nations to determine where he is placing his emphasis. The nations addressed by Jeremiah include those described in the following chart:

NATIONS ADDRESSED BY JEREMIAH		
NATION	**REFERENCE**	**TOTAL VERSES**
Egypt	46:1-28	28 verses
Philistia	47:1-7	7 verses
Moab	48:1-47	47 verses
Ammon	49:1-6	6 verses
Edom	49:7-22	16 verses
Damascus	49:23-27	5 verses
Kedar and Hazor	49:28-33	6 verses
Elam	49:34-39	6 verses
Babylon	50:1–51:64	110 verses

No chiastic structure is evident, and no nations are included twice in the list. The nations listed first and last are Egypt and Babylon, so these could be significant. (Egypt is the nation that supported Judah in her rebellion against Babylon, and Babylon is the nation that ultimately destroyed Judah.) The law of proportion supports the fact that Babylon is the dominant focus in the section. Of the 231 verses devoted to the nations, 110 of the verses (47.6 percent) focus on God's judgment against Babylon. But what does Jeremiah say about Babylon? Jeremiah provides two specific keys on the nature of the fulfillment one should expect for this prophecy. Each of these will be examined briefly.

TWO SPECIFIC KEYS ON THE NATURE OF THE FULFILLMENT OF JEREMIAH 50–51	
FIRST	The timing of the destruction.
SECOND	The results of the destruction.

The timing of the destruction

After announcing God's message "concerning Babylon, the land of the Chaldeans" (50:1), Jeremiah describes an attack that "will make her land an object of horror" (50:3). Beginning in 50:4, Jeremiah supplies a specific time marker to help identify *when* this destruction of Babylon will happen. The verse states:

> "In those days and at that time," declares the LORD, "the sons of Israel will come, *both* they and the sons of Judah as well; they will go along weeping as they go, and it will be the LORD their God they will seek.

In the days of Babylon's destruction Israel and Judah will experience a national regathering to the land. Jeremiah's use of the phrase, "In those days and at that time," is significant. The prophet uses this phrase in whole or in part nine times in his book, including twice in chapter 50. Of the seven occurrences outside Jeremiah 50, six of the occurrences have clear eschatological implications. The only exception is Jeremiah 5:18. We compare these references by means of the following chart:

JEREMIAH 3:16	"It shall be in those days when you are multiplied and increased in the land," declares the LORD, "they will no longer say, 'The ark of the covenant of the LORD.' And it will not come to mind, nor will they remember it, nor will they miss *it*, nor will it be made again."
JEREMIAH 3:18	In those days the house of Judah will walk with the house of Israel, and they will come together from the land of the north to the land that I gave your fathers as an inheritance.
JEREMIAH 31:29	In those days they will not say again, "The fathers have eaten sour grapes, And the children's teeth are set on edge."
JEREMIAH 31:33	"But this is the covenant which I will make with the house of Israel after those days," declares the LORD, "I will put My law within them and on their heart I will write it; and I will be their God, and they shall be My people."
JEREMIAH 33:15	In those days and at that time I will cause a righteous Branch of David to spring forth; and He shall execute justice and righteousness on the earth.
JEREMIAH 33:16	In those days Judah will be saved and Jerusalem will dwell in safety; and this is *the name* by which she will be called: the LORD is our righteousness.
JEREMIAH 50:4	"In those days and at that time," declares the LORD, "the sons of Israel will come, *both* they and the sons of Judah as well; they will go along weeping as they go, and it will be the LORD their God they will seek."
JEREMIAH 50:20	"In those days and at that time," declares the LORD, "search will be made for the iniquity of Israel, but there will be none; and for the sins of Judah, but they will not be found; for I will pardon those whom I leave as a remnant."

Jeremiah predicts that—in the days of Babylon's destruction—Israel and Judah will return to the land. A limited return to the land took place under Zerubbabel after Babylon fell to Cyrus, but is this the return to which Jeremiah refers here? The specifics of the passage seem to argue against the return under Zerubbabel being the fulfillment.

First, Jeremiah indicates that this return will involve "the sons of Israel . . ., *both* they and the sons of Judah as well" (50:4). This phrase links the remnants from both the northern and southern kingdoms and implies a return of all Jews to the land.

Eight times Jeremiah links future language ("in those days" or "days are coming") with a reuniting of Israel and Judah. Note these instances in the following chart:

JEREMIAH 3:18	In those days the house of Judah will walk with the house of Israel, and they will come together from the land of the north to the land that I gave your fathers as an inheritance.
JEREMIAH 23:5-6	"Behold, *the* days are coming," declares the LORD, "When I will raise up for David a righteous Branch; And He will reign as king and act wisely And do justice and righteousness in the land. "In His days Judah will be saved, And Israel will dwell securely; And this is His name by which He will be called, 'The LORD our righteousness.'"
JEREMIAH 30:3	"For behold, days are coming," declares the LORD, "when I will restore the fortunes of My people Israel and Judah." The LORD says, "I will also bring them back to the land that I gave to their forefathers and they shall possess it."
JEREMIAH 31:27	"Behold, days are coming," declares the LORD, "when I will sow the house of Israel and the house of Judah with the seed of man and with the seed of beast."

JEREMIAH 31:31	"Behold, days are coming," declares the LORD, "when I will make a new covenant with the house of Israel and with the house of Judah."
JEREMIAH 33:14	"Behold, days are coming," declares the LORD, "when I will fulfill the good word which I have spoken concerning the house of Israel and the house of Judah."
JEREMIAH 50:4	"In those days and at that time," declares the LORD, "the sons of Israel will come, *both* they and the sons of Judah as well; they will go along weeping as they go, and it will be the LORD their God they will seek."
JEREMIAH 50:20	"In those days and at that time," declares the LORD, "search will be made for the iniquity of Israel, but there will be none; and for the sins of Judah, but they will not be found; for I will pardon those whom I leave as a remnant."

Second, Jeremiah indicates that the return to the LORD following the destruction of Babylon will be both physical *and* spiritual. Not only will Israel and Judah return physically to the land, but "they will come that they may join themselves to the LORD *in* an everlasting covenant that will not be forgotten" (50:5). Jeremiah used the phrase "everlasting covenant" in 32:40 where it is parallel to the New Covenant. The return following the destruction of Babylon will bring a spiritual revival to the Jews.

Jeremiah adds additional information on this spiritual revival in 50:20:

> "In those days and at that time," declares the LORD, "search will be made for the iniquity of Israel, but there will be none; and for the sins of Judah, but they will not be found; for I will pardon those whom I leave as a remnant."

The return of Israel and Judah will be accompanied by a removal of their sin and guilt. This did *not* happen during the return under Zerubbabel. One need only read Ezra, Nehemiah, Haggai, Zechariah or Malachi to see the sin that plagued the remnant who had returned to the land. But Jeremiah's vision of Babylon's destruction is associated with a spiritual renewal among the people of Israel and Judah which is unprecedented in history.

The results of the destruction

In addition to providing some time elements associated with Babylon's fall, Jeremiah spends a great deal of time focusing on the results of the destruction that God will pour out on this city. Jeremiah makes at least four specific statements on the results of Babylon's fall.

They are categorized as follows:

1. Babylon's population will be killed.

50:21

"Against the land of Merathaim [i.e., "double rebellion"], go up against it,
And against the inhabitants of Pekod.
Slay and utterly destroy them," declares the LORD,
"And do according to all that I have commanded you."

50:26-27

Come to her from the farthest border;
Open up her barns,
Pile her up like heaps
And utterly destroy her,
Let nothing be left to her.
Put all her young bulls to the sword;
Let them go down to the slaughter!
Woe be upon them, for their day has come,
The time of their punishment.

50:29	Summon many against Babylon, All those who bend the bow: Encamp against her on every side, Let there be no escape. Repay her according to her work; According to all that she has done, *so* do to her; For she has become arrogant against the LORD, Against the Holy One of Israel.
50:30	"Therefore her young men will fall in her streets, And all her men of war will be silenced in that day," declares the LORD.
51:3-4	So do not spare her young men; Devote all her army to destruction. They will fall down slain in the land of the Chaldeans, And pierced through in their streets.
51:47	And her whole land will be put to shame And all her slain will fall in her midst.

2. Babylon's buildings will be plundered and her fortifications will be destroyed.

50:10	"Chaldea will become plunder; All who plunder her will have enough," declares the LORD.
50:15	She has given herself up, her pillars have fallen, Her walls have been torn down.
51:26	"They will not take from you *even* a stone for a corner Nor a stone for foundations, But you will be desolate forever," declares the LORD.

51:30
Their dwelling places are set on fire,
The bars of her *gates* are broken.

51:58
The broad wall of Babylon will be completely razed
And her high gates will be set on fire.

3. The city and country will remain uninhabited.

50:3
. . . and there will be no inhabitant in it. Both man and beast have wandered off, they have gone away!

50:13
Because of the indignation of the LORD she will not be inhabited,
But she will be completely desolate.

50:40
"As when God overthrew Sodom
And Gomorrah with its neighbors," declares the LORD,
"No man will live there,
Nor will *any* son of man reside in it."

51:29
So the land quakes and writhes,
For the purposes of the LORD against Babylon stand,
To make the land of Babylon
A desolation without inhabitants.

51:37
Babylon will become a heap of *ruins*, a haunt of jackals,
An object of horror and hissing, without inhabitants.

51:43
Her cities have become an object of horror,
A parched land and a desert,
A land in which no man lives
And through which no son of man passes.

51:64
Just so shall Babylon sink down and not rise again because of the calamity that I am going to bring upon her; and they will become exhausted.

4. Only those who flee from the city will be spared.

50:8	Wander away from the midst of Babylon And go forth from the land of the Chaldeans.
51:6	Flee from the midst of Babylon, And each of you save his life! Do not be destroyed in her punishment, For this is the LORD's time of vengeance; He is going to render recompense to her.
51:45	Come forth from her midst, My people, And each of you save yourselves From the fierce anger of the LORD.

If these descriptions are taken at face value, Babylon's fall results from a bloody battle that devastates the city. Only those wise enough to follow God's warning and flee before the battle begins will be spared. Once the battle is over Babylon will remain permanently desolate. These descriptions do not match Babylon's fall to Cyrus in 539 B.C. That fall was relatively peaceful and involved almost no death or destruction.

Two additional observations must be made regarding Jeremiah's description of the results of Babylon's fall. They are:

FIRST	Jeremiah compares Babylon's fall to that of Sodom and Gomorrah. In doing so, Jeremiah is identifying his destruction of Babylon with the one prophesied nearly a century earlier by Isaiah (Jer. 50:39-40; cf. Isa. 13:19-20).
SECOND	Jeremiah specifically commands those who are God's people to flee from Babylon before this attack begins. Daniel had access to the prophecies of Jeremiah (cf. Dan. 9:2), and he was in Babylon the night it fell to the Medo-Persians (Dan. 5:30). If Jeremiah's prophecy was being fulfilled that night, should not Daniel have already fled from Babylon? Either Daniel was unfamiliar with Jeremiah's warning or he chose to ignore Jeremiah's warning—or he did not identify Jeremiah's warning with the attack underway against Babylon in his day.

Jeremiah's prophecies were not fulfilled when Babylon fell to Cyrus in 539 B.C. The city was not destroyed, nor were the people killed. The city and surrounding land remained inhabited and productive. Israel and Judah did not combine a physical return to the land with a spiritual return to the LORD to be joined to Him in an everlasting covenant. Like Isaiah 13 and 14, either Jeremiah 50 and 51 were not intended to be taken literally or else this prophecy has not yet been fulfilled.

Zechariah 5:5-11

The third Old Testament prophecy relating to Babylon is Zechariah 5:5-11. Zechariah began his ministry to the remnant who had returned from Babylon with Zerubbabel and Joshua the high priest in 520 B.C. The group had returned to Jerusalem in 538 B.C., when Cyrus permitted the remnant to return and to build their temple. However, shortly after beginning the rebuilding of the temple in 536 B.C., the people halted their work because of local opposition. One purpose for God raising up the prophet Zechariah was to encourage the people to resume their work on the temple of the Lord (cf. Ezra 5:1). However, Zechariah looked beyond the temple to describe events leading up to both the first and second comings of the Messiah.

Zechariah's prophecy relating to Babylon is part of his series of eight night visions which form the first segment of his work (1:7–6:8). The prophecy itself is the seventh of the eight night visions. There is some evidence that these eight night visions are arranged in a chiastic structure.[70]

---

70 Baldwin, though she sees a slightly different chiastic structure in the eight night visions, notes the presence of chiasm throughout the book of Zechariah (Joyce G. Baldwin, *Haggai, Zechariah, Malachi, The Tyndale Old Testament Commentaries* [Downers Grove, IL: Inter-Varsity Press, 1972], pp. 80-81, 92-93). Instead of the pattern a b c d d' c' b' a' she sees the pattern a b b c c b b a (Ibid., p. 80).

A. The rider and horses among the myrtle trees (1:7-17)
(God is upset with the nations who have oppressed Israel)

B. The four horns and four craftsmen (1:18-21)
(The nations who have scattered Judah will be judged)

C. The man with the measuring line (2:1-13)
(Jerusalem will be physically restored)

D. Clean garments for the high priest (3:1-10)
(Israel will be blessed when the Branch comes)

D. The gold lampstand and two olive trees (4:1-14)
(God will empower His servants to complete the work)

C. The flying scroll (5:1-4)
(The land will be purged of sinners)

B. The woman in the basket (5:5-11)
(Evil will return to the land of Shinar)

A. The four chariots (6:1-8)
(God will conquer the nations who have opposed Israel)

In Zechariah's seventh night vision a measuring basket [lit. "ephah"] appears before the prophet. Inside the basket is a woman. The angel speaking with Zechariah identifies the woman in the basket: "This is Wickedness!" (Zech. 5:8). One key question is the location of this wickedness. Zechariah identifies it as "the iniquity [or "appearance" (NASB)] of the people throughout the land" (5:6, NIV).[71] The word for "land" can be translated "land or earth." Zechariah uses the word 40 times in his book. Excluding the passage in question, Zechariah uses "land" 21 times of the whole earth, 14 times to refer specifically to the land of Israel and four times to refer to other specific lands (Shinar, Hadrach, Egypt and Gilead). This personification of wickedness could refer to the wickedness residing in the land of Israel, or it could refer to the wickedness throughout the earth.

Whether Zechariah is referring to the wickedness in the land of Israel or the wickedness of the entire earth, one point is clear in the passage. This wickedness was being held in check in Zechariah's day. "A lead cover" had to be "lifted up" off the ephah before Zechariah could gaze at this personification of evil (5:7). As soon as he had seen the woman who represented evil and she had been identified, "he threw her down into the middle of the ephah and cast the lead weight on its opening" (5:8). Whatever this wickedness represented, God was not allowing it to escape in Zechariah's day.

As Zechariah gazed at the basket it was carried away by two additional angelic beings. Zechariah turned to his angelic guide and asked,

---

71 The difference between "appearance/resemblance" (NASB, KJV) and "iniquity" (NIV) is based on a textual variation. Ken Barker presents a succinct summary of the problem and the likely solution. "('*enam*) presents a text-critical problem. As it stands, it means 'their eye' [i.e., their appearance), which does not yield a good sense (cf. the parallel in v. 8, where the woman in the basket is interpreted as wickedness personified). NIV, probably correctly, follows one Hebrew MS, the LXX, and the Syriac. . . . (The pronominal suffix refers to the people, perhaps with special reference to the godless rich.) The only significant variation between these two readings is the waw instead of the yod. Even here it should be borne in mind that in many ancient Hebrew MSS the only perceptible difference between the two letters is the length of the downward stroke. A long yod and a short waw are virtually indistinguishable" (Kenneth L. Barker, "Zechariah," in *The Expositor's Bible Commentary*, vol. 7, *Daniel–Minor Prophets* [Grand Rapids: Zondervan Publishing House, 1985], p. 635).

"Where are they taking the ephah?" (5:10). What was to be the final destiny of this container of evil? The angel's answer was very precise: "To build a temple for her in the land of Shinar" (5:11).

Shinar occurs eight times in the Old Testament in the New American Standard Bible. Four of the occurrences are in Genesis where it is associated with the city of Babel established by Nimrod following the flood (Gen. 10:10), with the tower of Babel (Gen. 11:2) and with the coalition of nations threatening the land God promised to Abram (Gen. 14:1, 9). Joshua 7:21 uses it to describe the "mantle" that Achan "coveted." Isaiah 11:11 uses it in a list of places from which God will regather His people in the Messianic age. Daniel 1:2 identifies Shinar as the location to which Daniel and his friends were carried by Nebuchadnezzar. In short, every occurrence of Shinar identifies it as the land associated with Babylon.[72] Zechariah saw wickedness flying back to Babylon.

The angels were taking wickedness to Babylon, "To build a temple for her" (Zech. 5:11). The NIV uses the word "house" instead of "temple."[73] It seems to me that the translation "temple" presupposes a religious character that is not obvious from the text. While *beit* can be translated "temple," its basic meaning is "house" or "dwelling place."[74] The point of Zechariah's vision is that a new abode for wickedness will again be set up in Shinar. "When it is prepared, she will be set there on her own pedestal" (5:11).

Zechariah penned these words 19 years after Babylon's fall to Cyrus. If the prophecies of Isaiah and Jeremiah had been fulfilled in the fall of Babylon, then Zechariah's words seem out of place. However, if the

---

72 Barker concludes that Shinar "roughly corresponded to ancient Babylonia" (Barker, "Zechariah," p. 635).

73 Baldwin assumes the reference must be to a temple. "Another temple will be erected, perhaps a ziggurat like the tower of Babel. . . ." (Baldwin, *Haggai, Zechariah, Malachi*, p. 129). Barker, though more tentative in his identification, still suggests that the word is "perhaps referring to a temple or ziggurat" (Barker, "Zechariah," p. 635).

74 Francis Brown, S. R. Driver, and Charles A. Briggs, *A Hebrew and English Lexicon of the Old Testament*, s.v., "*Beyt*," pp. 108-10.

prophecies of Isaiah and Jeremiah were not fulfilled when Cyrus captured the city, then Zechariah's vision could relate in some way to those earlier prophecies. God was holding wickedness in check, but there would come a time when wickedness would once again have a dwelling place in Babylon.

In closing, two specific points of note must be made regarding Zechariah 5:5-11.

First, Zechariah personifies the evil that will one day dwell again in Shinar as a woman. Could this be the underlying imagery behind John's description of Babylon in Revelation 17?

Second, if Zechariah's eight night visions are in a chiastic structure, then the end-time evil in Shinar (5:5-11) is parallel in some way to the vision of four evil empires ("horns" [Zech. 1:18, 19, 21]) that oppress Judah until they are removed by the Lord. Zechariah's four nations are suspiciously parallel to Daniel's four Gentile powers that control Jerusalem during "the times of the Gentiles" (Luke 21:24; cf. Dan. 2; 7).

The final Gentile power (the fourth horn) of Zechariah would be parallel to the "feet of iron and clay" of Daniel 2:34 or "the fourth beast" of Daniel 7:23. But how could wickedness in Shinar (Zech. 5) be associated with the fourth Gentile power (Zech. 1)? Once again Revelation 17 may provide the answer. John describes the evil woman named "BABYLON" (Rev. 17:5) astride the "beast" (Rev. 17:3) that is parallel to the fourth beast of Daniel 7. Both Babylon and the fourth empire are associated in John's end-time vision, as Zechariah's chiastic structure would suggest.

But while these parallels are interesting, one cannot make any positive identification from Zechariah alone. Having examined the three key Old Testament prophecies on Babylon, this study must now turn to John's vision of Babylon in the book of Revelation. It is this writer's belief that John pulls together the threads of numerous Old Testament prophecies, including the prophecies of Babylon.

Revelation 17–18

One key factor in interpreting God's prophetic program is the identification of the eschatological Babylon described by the Apostle John in Revelation 17 and 18. These two chapters occupy a significant portion of the book of Revelation, and they provide a graphic account of God's future judgment on evil. However, interpreters face many problems in trying to identify the end-time system of evil pictured in these two chapters. What is the "Babylon" described by John in these two chapters?

The relationship between Revelation 17 and 18 is crucial to a proper understanding of the Babylon referred to in both. Do Revelation 17 and 18 separately describe two distinct Babylons, as many Bible teachers have long held? Those who hold such a position believe that Revelation 17 describes *ecclesiastical* Babylon, which will be destroyed by the Antichrist in the middle of the tribulation period, and that Revelation 18 describes *economic* Babylon, the capital of the Antichrist that will be destroyed at the end of the tribulation period. However, do these two chapters unite in presenting the fall of a single Babylon, whatever that Babylon might be? These questions must be answered.

The distinctions between the chapters

Any attempt to understand the relationship between Revelation 17 and 18 must take into account several distinctions that appear between the two chapters. Primarily because of these distinctions many expositors argue for the identification of two Babylons in the chapters. Four arguments against the unity of the two chapters have been advanced by various authors.

Those arguments are listed in the following chart:

FOUR ARGUMENTS AGAINST THE UNITY OF REVELATION 17 AND 18

1. Different settings

2. Different destroyers

3. Different responses

4. Different character

Let us consider each of those arguments carefully:

1. Different settings

The first difficulty faced in trying to identify the subject of these two chapters is the different settings for each chapter. The chapters tell of two visions introduced by two different angels. Chapter 18 begins, "After these things I saw another angel coming down from heaven." The problem centers on the expression "after these things" (*meta tauta*). John used this phrase a number of times in the book of Revelation, and several times it indicated a major break between events. "The phrase is of great importance in Revelation 1:19 and 4:1.... The phrase ... suggests that after the events described in Revelation 17 have run their course, the judgment of Babylon [in chapter 18] has still to occur."[75]

Does use of the phrase "after these things" (*meta tauta*) demand a gap between these chapters? John used this phrase 10 times in the book of

---

75 Kenneth W. Allen, "The Rebuilding and Destruction of Babylon," *Bibliotheca Sacra* 133 (January–March, 1976):25.

Revelation. Six times it occurs with a word of perception, and four times it does not. When the phrase is used with a verb of perception ("I saw," "I heard") it simply indicates the time sequence in which the visions were revealed to John. This is the temporal use of *meta tauta*. In this usage John was indicating that the time sequence was in his observation of the visions and not necessarily in the unfolding of future events. When John wanted to indicate a gap of time in future events, he did not include a verb of perception. The 10 occurrences are as follows:

TEMPORAL USE
4:1A — After these things I looked, and behold, a door *standing* open in heaven.
7:1 — After this I saw four angels standing at the four corners of the earth, holding back the four winds of the earth. . . .
7:9 — After these things I looked, and behold, a great multitude which no one could count. . . .
15:5 — After these things I looked, and the temple of the tabernacle of testimony in heaven was opened.
18:1 — After these things I saw another angel coming down from heaven, having great authority, and the earth was illumined with his glory.
19:1 — After these things I heard something like a loud voice of a great multitude in heaven. . . .

	ESCHATOLOGICAL USE
1:19	Therefore write the things which you have seen, and the things which are, and the things which will take place after these things.
4:1B	Come up here, and I will show you what must take place after these things.
9:12	The first woe is past; behold, two woes are still coming after these things.
20:3	And he threw him into the abyss, and shut *it* and sealed *it* over him, so that he would not deceive the nations any longer, until the thousand years were completed; after these things he must be released for a short time.

The four references not associated with verbs of perception do indicate chronological distinctions between future events. However, those with verbs of perception only indicate the order in which the parts of the vision are viewed by John. Thus, the mere presence of *meta tauta* in Revelation 18:1 does not indicate a chronological distinction between the chapters. It only shows that the events revealed to John by the second angel were shown *after* he had viewed the woman on the beast.

2. Different destroyers

A second alleged distinction between Revelation 17 and 18 is the apparent difference between the destroyers of Babylon. The Babylon of chapter 17 is destroyed by kings whereas the Babylon of chapter 18 is destroyed by fire. The destruction of the "harlot Babylon" occurs in

17:16, which states, "The ten horns which you saw, and the beast, these will hate the harlot and will make her desolate and naked. . . . " The destruction of the *commercial* Babylon occurs in 18:8, which states, "For this reason in one day her plagues will come, pestilence and mourning and famine, and she will be burned up with fire; for the Lord God who judges her is strong."

A second distinction in destroyers between the chapters has also been suggested. The destruction is a contrast not only between the 10 kings and fire, but also between a destruction by man and a destruction by God. "The great harlot is destroyed by the ten kings (Rev. 17:16b); but the city of Babylon [chap. 18] is destroyed by God. . . ."[76]

If these two distinctions are valid, then any attempt to view the chapters as a unit will be doomed to failure. However, are these distinctions consistent with the text? A careful evaluation shows that they are not. For example, it is held that the "harlot Babylon" of chapter 17 was destroyed by men while the *commercial* Babylon of chapter 18 was destroyed by fire. This does not explain 17:16b, which says, "These . . . will burn her up with fire." Thus, in reality, Babylon is destroyed by fire in both chapters.

The distinction is made between man's destruction (ch. 17) and God's destruction (ch. 18). This, however, fails to account for 17:17, which explains the destruction of the harlot by the beast and 10 kings as stemming initially from God. "For God has put it in their hearts to execute His purpose by having a common purpose. . . ." Both chapters do ascribe the destruction to God.

Revelation 17 and 18 are more similar than many expositors believe. This chart shows that, in fact, the chapters do not have different destroyers.

---

76 Ibid., p. 26.

	REVELATION 17	REVELATION 18
OBJECT OF DESTRUCTION	BABYLON THE GREAT. (17:5)	The great city, Babylon, the strong city! (18:10)
INSTRUMENT OF DESTRUCTION	And the ten horns which you saw, and the beast. (17:16)	(not given)
MEANS OF DESTRUCTION	Will burn her up with fire. (17:16)	She will be burned up with fire. (18:8)
SOURCE OF DESTRUCTION	For God has put it in their hearts to execute His purpose. (17:17)	For the Lord God who judges her is strong. (18:8)

This chart shows that the only distinction to be found is the instrument of destruction. Chapter 17 focuses on the human instrument while chapter 18 does not. If the chapters are viewed synthetically, the alleged distinctions between the destroyers vanish. In their place stands a unified whole, with each chapter focusing on a different aspect of one destruction.

3. Different responses

A third distinction between Revelation 17 and 18 is the different responses to the destruction that are ascribed to the kings of each chapter.[77] The response of the kings in chapter 17 is recorded in 17:16.

> And the ten horns which you saw, and the beast, these will hate the harlot and will make her desolate and naked, and will eat her flesh and will burn her up with fire.

---

77 In observing these different responses, Tenney comments: "Why should the kings both hate her and then bewail her fate at their hands? Perhaps the explanation lies in the difference between religious and commercial Babylon" (Merrill C. Tenney, *Interpreting Revelation* [Grand Rapids: Wm. B. Eerdmans Publishing Co., 1957], p. 85).

The "ten horns" are identified in 17:12 as "ten kings."

In contrast to the hatred and destruction of Babylon by the kings of chapter 17, the kings of chapter 18 respond by mourning:

> And the kings of the earth, who committed *acts of* immorality and lived sensuously with her, will weep and lament over her when they see the smoke of her burning. (Rev. 18:9)

Two opposite responses are attributed to the kings of each chapter. However, there is an explanation apart from assuming two Babylons. An alternative is to assume that two distinct groups of kings are in view in the two chapters. As Ladd has observed, "The kings of the earth [in 18:9-10] are to be distinguished from the 10 kings who joined with the beast to war against the Lamb (17:12-14)."[78] Thus, the kings who hate Babylon (17:16) are those "ten kings" who unite with the beast to plot her overthrow. The remaining "kings of the earth" (18:9-10) are engaged in commerce with Babylon, so they mourn when their source of revenue is destroyed. This view is consistent with the particulars of the text but still seeks to harmonize the two chapters.

4. Different character

The final difference between the chapters is the different character of each Babylon that is described. Chapter 17 is said to be religious in nature while chapter 18 is more commercial. Many feel that these differences can best be explained by the existence of two Babylons in the chapters. "Revelation 17 sets forth a religious power centered at the seven-hilled city of Rome exerting control over all people until the Antichrist has no further use for its existence, while the city of Babylon [chapter 18] is a great commercial center controlling trade and commerce on a worldwide scale."[79]

---

78 George Eldon Ladd, *A Commentary on the Revelation of John* (Grand Rapids: Wm. B. Eerdmans Publishing Co., 1972), p. 235.

79 Allen, "The Rebuilding and Destruction of Babylon," p. 26.

Is there a difference in character between these chapters? Chapter 17 contains a vision with an interpretation. Babylon is referred to in the vision as a woman riding a beast. In a sense a vision is a word picture. However, the fact that something is presented in a pictorial fashion does not mean that it has no concrete reality. The nation Israel is no less Israel because it is pictured as a woman in Revelation 12. Likewise Babylon is no less Babylon even though it is pictured as a harlot. The key to the vision in chapter 17 is the Divine interpretation given in 17:7-18. This gives the concrete reality behind the vision. What then is the truth about the harlot? Does she represent a religious system, a spiritual prostitute? Revelation 17:18 suggests that the answer is no: "The woman whom you saw is the great city, which reigns over the kings of the earth."

Babylon is pictured as a woman in chapter 17. However, when God identifies the woman to John, He tells John that the woman represents a *city*. Therefore, the entire argument crumbles because the chapters do contain the same character. Both chapters are talking about a city. This may not automatically mean that the Babylons in the two chapters are identical, but it certainly cannot be used to argue against such an identification.

Four distinctions between chapters 17 and 18 have been examined. Not one of the four distinctions contains compelling evidence for making a division between the chapters. The different settings are merely temporal aspects connected with John's viewing of the visions. Supposed differences between the destroyers vanish when the chapters are viewed synthetically. The different responses by the kings are explained by the existence of two distinct groups of kings within the chapters, and the alleged different character of the chapters actually vanishes when the spotlight of God's interpretation is focused on the woman in chapter 17.

The specific parallels between the chapters

A detailed examination of Revelation 17 and 18 uncovers a number of parallels between the two chapters. These can best be viewed in chart form.

	REVELATION 17	REVELATION 18
THE NAME IS THE SAME	BABYLON THE GREAT. (17:5)	Babylon the great! (18:2)
THE IDENTITY IS THE SAME	The woman whom you saw is the great city. (17:18)	Woe, woe, the great city, Babylon, the strong city! (18:10)

However one wishes to interpret the Babylon of Revelation 17, he or she must acknowledge that the Divine identification of the prostitute in Revelation 17 is a city, not a mystical system. These two chapters each present a city that has the same name in the same general context. The most natural interpretation is to take the cities as identical unless there is compelling evidence to the contrary.

	REVELATION 17	REVELATION 18
THE CLOTHING IS THE SAME	The woman was clothed in purple and scarlet, and adorned with gold and precious stones and pearls. (17:4a)	Saying, "Woe, woe, the great city, she who was clothed in fine linen and purple and scarlet, and adorned with gold and precious stones and pearls." (18:16)

BOTH HOLD A CUP	Having in her hand a gold cup full of abominations and of the unclean things of her immorality. (17:4b)	Pay her back even as she has paid, and give back *to her* double according to her deeds; in the cup which she has mixed, mix twice as much for her. (18:6)

Each Babylon is identified as a city, and both are described in the same fashion. Apart from the addition of "fine linen" in Revelation 18:12, both cities are arrayed with exactly the same materials. Also both are associated with a cup that each possesses. Instead of seeing two different cities that happen to have the same name and the same description, it is easier to assume the existence of only one city.

The deeds

	REVELATION 17	REVELATION 18
THE RELATIONSHIP TO KINGS IS THE SAME	With whom the kings of the earth committed *acts of* immorality. (17:2)	The kings of the earth have committed *acts of* immorality with her. (18:3)
THE RELATIONSHIP TO THE NATIONS IS THE SAME	And those who dwell on the earth were made drunk with the wine of her immorality. (17:2)	For all the nations have drunk of the wine of the passion of her immorality. (18:3)
THE RELATIONSHIP TO BELIEVERS IS THE SAME	And I saw the woman drunk with the blood of the saints, and with the blood of the witnesses of Jesus. When I saw her, I wondered greatly. (17:6)	And in her was found the blood of prophets and of saints and of all who have been slain on the earth. (18:24)

The Babylons in both chapters perform the same functions. Each commits fornication with the kings of the earth and causes all the nations of the earth to fall into a drunken stupor. Each also persecutes God's remnant who stand in opposition to evil. One cannot distinguish a political Babylon from a religious Babylon through a comparison of their deeds because the deeds are identical.

The destruction

	REVELATION 17	REVELATION 18
THE MEANS OF DESTRUCTION IS THE SAME	These will hate the harlot and will make her desolate and naked, and will eat her flesh and will burn her up with fire. (17:16)	She will be burned up with fire. (18:8)
THE SOURCE OF THE DESTRUCTION IS THE SAME	For God has put it in their hearts to execute His purpose. (17:17)	God has remembered her iniquities. . . . The Lord God who judges her is strong. (18:5, 8)

These final similarities surround the destruction of both Babylons. Physically both are destroyed by fire. And in both instances God is the ultimate source of destruction.

The parallels between the chapters are impressive. Each chapter refers to a city with the same name. Each describes a city in the same fashion. Each mentions a city that performs the same deeds, and each refers to a city that is destroyed in the same manner. These descriptions, going beyond mere similarity, point toward unity. Two distinct cities could hardly be described in such a similar way. It is better to view the chapters as two descriptions of the same city.

The larger context

The larger context in which Revelation 17 and 18 are positioned also underscores the parallelism between the chapters. The larger context actually begins in 14:6, which first predicts an "angel flying in midheaven" proclaiming proleptically, "Fallen, fallen is Babylon the great, she who has made all the nations drink of the wine of the passion of her immorality" (14:8). Several of the phrases used here are later repeated in Revelation 17 and 18. The title "BABYLON THE GREAT" is used in all three chapters; and the proclamation "Fallen, fallen is Babylon the great" is repeated in 18:2. The reference to the nations being intoxicated "with the wine of her immorality" is also found in 17:2 (cf. 18:3). This one proclamation is fulfilled by chapters 17 and 18, and yet there is only one Babylon in view in 14:8.

The next appearance of Babylon occurs during the outpouring of the seventh bowl in chapter 16. Part of the judgment is that, "Babylon the great was remembered before God, to give her the cup of the wine of His fierce wrath" (16:19). Again only one Babylon is in view. Immediately after this pronouncement John recorded the destruction of "BABYLON THE GREAT" in chapters 17–18. What is important is that chapters 17 and 18 are an expansion of 16:19, which seems to refer to the destruction of a city called Babylon—which is pictured as a literal city.

The larger context begins before chapters 17 and 18, but it does not end there. The subject of the fall of Babylon extends beyond these chapters into chapter 19. Revelation 19:1-5 presents the "Hallelujah Chorus" in heaven following the destruction of Babylon. As Ladd has noted, "The first paragraph of chapter nineteen continues the celebration of the fall of Babylon and consists of a song of thanksgiving in heaven that God had judged the great harlot."[80]

---

80   Ladd, *A Commentary on the Revelation of John*, p. 244.

Chapter 19 begins with the phrase, "After these things"—referring to the visions of chapters 17 and 18. In 18:20 the author calls on heaven to "rejoice over" the fall of Babylon; chapter 19 describes heaven's response to that call. The first part of the heavenly praise focuses on the prostitute of chapter 17. The multitude says, "He has judged the great harlot who was corrupting the earth with her immorality, and HE HAS AVENGED THE BLOOD OF HIS BOND-SERVANTS ON HER" (19:2). In response to the angels' call to "rejoice over" the fall of Babylon in 18:20 the heavens do respond—with a song of praise for the "judgment" of the "harlot." The implication is that the harlot of chapter 17 and the Babylon of chapter 18 are identical.

The song of praise continues in 19:3, which says, "And a second time they said, 'Hallelujah! HER SMOKE RISES UP FOREVER AND EVER.'" The reference to the smoldering city is drawn from chapter 18, in which the kings of the earth and the shipmasters are said to look on "the smoke of her burning" (18:9, 18). The praise song in heaven over the fall of Babylon incorporates elements from both chapter 17 and chapter 18, and yet it seems to be a song celebrating just one fall and doing so in response to the command of 18:20. Again this larger context can be understood best if chapters 17 and 18 are viewed as a unit that looks forward to the destruction of a single city of Babylon.

The interpretive keys within the chapters

John's picture of a prostitute astride a scarlet beast in chapter 17 could be entitled *Beauty on the Beast*. The vision is described in the first six verses and then interpreted in the next 12 verses. Chapter 18 focuses on the response of individuals to Babylon's destruction. Within the two chapters are four interpretive keys that are crucial to the identification of Babylon.

The description of Babylon as a harlot

The first interpretive key is the descriptive identification of Babylon in 17:1 as "the great harlot who sits on many waters." This allusion to a prostitute has caused many to identify Babylon as a false religious system. "The frequently recurring allusion to harlotry . . . is an echo of the Old Testament prophets, who used the term to describe the infidelity of man to God, especially in connection with idolatry."[81]

Admittedly the figure of a prostitute was used in the Old Testament to describe idolatry. However, the figure was also used in the Old Testament to show more than just religious apostasy. Literal cities such as Nineveh (Nah. 3:4), Tyre (Isa. 23:16-17) and Jerusalem (Ezek. 16:15) were characterized as being prostitutes. "In the context of Revelation 17 and 18 the image is not that of religious profligacy but of the prostitution of all that is right and noble for the questionable ends of power and luxury."[82]

Babylon is identified as a prostitute. But the reference is not to her spiritual nature. Rather the focus is on the prostitution of her values for economic gain. The figure of a harlot was never applied to a religious system *only*. It was always used to describe a city or nation (Jerusalem, Israel, Samaria, Nineveh or Tyre). Why did John describe Babylon as a harlot? One reason was to contrast Babylon and Jerusalem. Two cities in Revelation are described as "great"—Jerusalem and Babylon. John, through his use of literary parallels, highlights the contrast between the destruction of Babylon and the final triumph of Jerusalem.

---

81   Merrill C. Tenney, *Interpreting Revelation*, p. 83.

82   Robert H. Mounce, *The Book of Revelation* (Grand Rapids: Wm. B. Eerdmans Publishing Co., 1977), p. 307.

DESTRUCTION OF BABYLON REVELATION 17:1, 3-5, 18	ESTABLISHMENT OF JERUSALEM REVELATION 21:9-11, 27
Then one of the seven angels who had the seven bowls	Then one of the seven angels who had the seven bowls full of the seven last plagues
came and spoke with me...	came and spoke with me, saying,
"Come here, I will show you the judgment of the great harlot who sits on many waters. . . ."	"Come here, I will show you the bride, the wife of the Lamb."
And he carried me away in the Spirit into a wilderness. . . .	And he carried me away in the Spirit to a great and high mountain . . .
The woman was clothed in purple and scarlet, and adorned with gold and precious stones and pearls . . .	having the glory of God. Her brilliance was like a very costly stone, as a stone of crystal-clear jasper.
and on her forehead a name *was* written, a mystery, "BABYLON THE GREAT, THE MOTHER OF HARLOTS AND OF THE ABOMINATIONS OF THE EARTH. . . ." The woman whom you saw is the great city, which reigns over the kings of the earth.	and [he] showed me the holy city, Jerusalem, coming down out of heaven from God. . . . and nothing unclean, and no one who practices abomination and lying, shall ever come into it. . . .

The explanation of Babylon as a "mystery"

The second interpretive key centers on the name written on the harlot's forehead. More specifically, it revolves around the explanation of the word *mysterion* in 17:5. Babylon is described as "a mystery."

Two problems must be resolved before this interpretive key can be properly understood.

The first is the determination of the grammatical relationship between the word *mysterion* and the title of the woman. According to Robertson, *mysterion* could be taken "either in apposition with *onoma* ['name'] or as part of the inscription on her [i.e., the prostitute's] forehead."[83] So either John could be saying that the name on the woman is "MYSTERY, BABYLON THE GREAT" (Rev. 17:5, KJV) or he could be saying that the name, "BABYLON THE GREAT," which is written on the woman's forehead (Rev. 17:5) is a mystery. Of the two possibilities, the second offers the best explanation within the context. Whenever the woman is named elsewhere in the chapters she is simply called "Babylon the great" (14:8; cf. 16:19; 18:2), not "MYSTERY, BABYLON THE GREAT" (Rev. 17:5, KJV).

The second problem that must be resolved is the exact nature of the mystery. In what sense is this Babylon a mystery? Many feel that the occurrence of *mysterion* means that Babylon is to be interpreted symbolically or figuratively.[84] However, the idea of equating *mysterion* with something mystical cannot be borne out in the New Testament usage of the word. The word *mysterion* does not denote the quality or character of the truth; rather it focuses on the availability of that truth.

Whereas "mystery" may mean—and in contemporary usage often does mean—a secret for which no answer can be found, this is not at all the connotation of the term *mysterion* in classical and Biblical Greek. In the New Testament, *mysterion* signifies a secret which is being, or even has been, revealed, which is also Divine in scope and needs to be made known by God to men through His Spirit. In this way the term comes very close to the New Testament word *apokalypsis*, "revelation." *Mysterion* is a temporary secret, which once revealed is known and understood—a secret no longer.[85]

---

83 Archibald Thomas Robertson, *Word Pictures in the New Testament*, 6 vols. (Nashville: Broadman Press, 1933), 6:430.

84 Ibid. Robertson wrote, "In either case the meaning is the same, that the name Babylon is to be interpreted mystically or spiritually (cf. *pneymatiks* 11:8) for Rome."

85 *The New Bible Dictionary*, 1974 ed., s.v. "Mystery," by S. S. Smalley, p. 856. Barker agrees with Smalley. "The Greek term, however, refers to a mystery of divine nature that remains hidden from

Calling the harlot's name a mystery does not automatically mean a spiritual or mystical system of evil as opposed to a literal *brick and mortar* city. By designating Babylon as a "mystery," God was indicating to John that the vision being given had not been made known before. To understand the "mystery" in its context one must examine 17:7-18, for in these verses God reveals the meaning and significance of the vision.

The "mystery" that John saw was two end-time world powers (the prostitute and the beast on which she was riding) in existence at the same time. The Old Testament did point to the rise of Rome, which was to rule the world just prior to the establishment of Christ's kingdom (cf. Dan. 2:40-45; 7:23-27; 9:26-27). However, the Old Testament also predicted the restoration of Babylon as a major power in God's future prophetic program (cf. Isa. 13–14; Jer. 50–51; Zech. 5:5-11). But how could both of these empires exist simultaneously and fit into God's program for the world? That was the "mystery" revealed to John. After viewing the vision (Rev. 17:1-6), the angel said to John, "I will tell you the mystery (*mysterion*) of the woman and of the beast that carries her" (17:7).

The identification of Babylon as a city.

There is no lack of opinion concerning the identification of the prostitute called Babylon. However, most of the identifications do not begin with the Divine interpretation of the vision given at the end of chapter 17. In 17:18 the angel interpreted the harlot to John: "The woman whom you saw is the great city, which reigns over the kings of the earth." Whatever else is said about the prostitute, God identifies her first as a city, not an ecclesiastical system.

The Divine interpretive key in Revelation 17:18 identifies the Babylon of chapter 17 as a city. It is a city of worldwide importance, for it is said to

human beings because their normal powers of comprehension are insufficient. Nonetheless, these mysteries are intended for human beings and when known prove profitable to them" *(The International Standard Bible Encyclopedia,* 1986 ed., s.v., "Mystery," by G. W. Berker, 3:451-52).

reign over the other "kings of the earth." It is true that the identification can go beyond the city to the system it controls. However, the interpretation given to John focused only on the identification of Babylon as a city. In the secularized West, society separates church and state, but no such separation existed in antiquity. Babylon may have a religious aspect (for example, she persecutes believers), but this does not argue against Babylon being a literal city.

The location of Babylon on seven hills

The beast on which the woman is sitting is described as "having seven heads" (17:3). When the angel interpreted this part of the vision to John he said, "Here is the mind which has wisdom. The seven heads are seven mountains on which the woman sits, and they are seven kings; five have fallen, one is, the other has not yet come; and when he comes, he must remain a little while" (17:9-10). What are the "seven mountains" on which the woman is sitting? The traditional understanding is that they refer to the city of Rome, known in John's day as the seven-hilled city.[86]

This view that the "seven hills" (Rev. 17:9, NIV) refer to Rome has some serious flaws.

The first flaw is the assumed relationship between the woman and the hills. The seven heads are associated with the beast, not the woman. There is a distinction between the woman and the beast; and it is the beast that has the seven heads. The angel said, "I will tell you the mystery of the woman and of the beast that carries her, which has the seven heads and the ten horns" (17:7). If the seven hills refer to Rome, then the most that can be determined is that the Antichrist's empire will be centered in the city of Rome. It does not identify the location of the prostitute because she is not an organic part of the beast.

---

86 Mounce writes, "There is little doubt that a first-century reader would understand this reference in any way other than as a reference to Rome, the city built upon seven hills" (Mounce, *The Book of Revelation*, pp. 313-14).

Some might argue that the harlot is still to be associated with the city of seven hills because they are described in 17:9 as "seven mountains on which the woman sits." However, the prostitute's sitting on the seven hills is a reference to her *control or influence*, not to her location. In 17:1 the woman is sitting "on many waters." These are interpreted in 17:15 as "peoples and multitudes and nations and tongues." The purpose of this part of the vision is not to show Babylon's location or else the city would have to be parceled out throughout the world. Rather, the prostitute sitting on the waters is a reference to her control or influence over all the nations of the world. The woman is also said to sit on the entire beast (17:3). This would go beyond just the seven heads to include the Antichrist and the kings allied with him. Again the reference is to her control or influence, not to her location. If the harlot's sitting clearly indicates control or influence twice in the chapter, is it not inconsistent to give that same figure a different meaning when it occurs for a third time? It is far more consistent to view the harlot's sitting as indicative of her control over the seven mountains, rather than having it point to her physical location.

Even if the seven hills are taken as a reference to Rome, that identification cannot be used to associate the harlot with Rome. The woman and the seven heads are distinct; and the position of the woman indicates control, not location. However, there is evidence to believe that the seven hills could refer to something other than the city of Rome.

To understand properly the symbolism of the seven mountains one must go beyond the Greco-Roman society in which John wrote to the Jewish heritage in which he was raised. John was a Jew, and the book of Revelation must be interpreted in light of the Old Testament. As Jenkins has said, "The book of Revelation is the most thoroughly Jewish in its language and imagery of any New Testament book. This book speaks not the language of Paul, but of the Old Testament prophets Isaiah, Ezekiel, and Daniel."[87]

---

87 Ferrel Jenkins, *The Old Testament in the Book of Revelation* (Grand Rapids: Baker Book House,

To understand the seven mountains one must go to the Old Testament to see how this symbol was used. The word *mountain* was often a symbolic reference to a kingdom or national power. The following Old Testament passages show this usage of the word:

> Now it will come about that
> In the last days
> The mountain of the house of the LORD
> Will be established as the chief of the mountains,
> And will be raised above the hills;
> And all the nations will stream to it. (Isa. 2:2)

> "Behold, I am against you, O destroying mountain,
> Who destroys the whole earth," declares the LORD,
> "And I will stretch out My hand against you,
> And roll you down from the crags,
> And I will make you a burnt out mountain." (Jer. 51:25)
> [The Lord is here speaking to the nation of Babylon; see Jer. 50:1. Note that Jeremiah 50 and 51 are quoted extensively in Revelation 17 and 18.]

> But the stone that struck the statue became a great mountain and filled the whole earth. . . . In the days of those kings the God of heaven will set up a kingdom which will never be destroyed, and *that* kingdom will not be left for another people; it will crush and put an end to all these kingdoms, but it will itself endure forever. (Dan. 2:35, 44) [Note that God identified the mountain as the everlasting kingdom He will set up.]

The figure of a mountain is used in the Old Testament to refer to a kingdom. However, there is yet another reason for identifying the seven mountains in Revelation 17 as a reference to seven kingdoms. This interpretation is to be preferred because it best explains the dual identification of the seven heads as *both* mountains and kings.

If the seven mountains are applied to Rome, then the seven kings must be seven rulers of Rome. However, there is some difficulty in relating the known history of Rome's rulers to the seven kings of the vision. One

1976), p. 22.

must leave out three Roman emperors (Galba, Otho and Vitellius) to have the history of Rome fit John's chronology. But this is not sound interpretation. "Such a procedure is arbitrary, for Galba, Otho and Vitellius, unimportant as they may have been, were bona fide emperors and were recognized as such by ancient historians."[88]

The Divine interpretation associates each head with both a mountain and a king. This can best be explained by viewing the "mountain" as a figure of speech that refers to a kingdom and the king who was ruling it.

This relationship is most clearly illustrated in Daniel's interpretation of Nebuchadnezzar's dream in Daniel 2. "You are the head of gold. After you there will arise another kingdom inferior to you" (Dan. 2:38b-39). Daniel wrote that the head of gold was a *king*, but that the breast and arms of silver were another *kingdom*. Daniel was obviously viewing the kingdom of Babylon as personified in the king that stood before him. Thus he could switch from the king to the kingdom with no inconsistency. The Apostle John is using the ideas of kingdoms and rulers in the same way. The seven heads which are identified as "mountains" and "kings" in Revelation 17:9-10 refer to seven empires and their kings rather than to the city of Rome.

The four interpretive keys within Revelation 17 and 18 provide vital information on the identity of Babylon. Babylon is first and foremost a literal city that will dominate the world. It will be characterized as a harlot that prostitutes her moral values for material luxury. The entire city is viewed as a mystery in that her future position, relationship to the Antichrist and ultimate destruction by the Antichrist had not been known before John's vision. Evidently Babylon will exert influence or control over seven nations, the Antichrist's growing empire and—eventually—the entire earth.

These keys do not unlock some mystical system of religion that will infiltrate the world. Rather, they open the door of prophecy on a brick-and-mortar city intoxicated with power and luxury. The Babylon in these

---

88 Ladd, *A Commentary on the Revelation of John*, p. 229.

chapters, though it might have religious aspects, is one that will exist geographically and politically.

FOUR INTERPRETIVE KEYS WITHIN REVELATION 17–18	
FIRST	The description of Babylon as a harlot.
SECOND	The explanation of Babylon as a "mystery."
THIRD	The identification of Babylon as a city.
FOURTH	The location of Babylon on seven hills.

The Relationship to the Old Testament Prophecies on Babylon

An examination of Revelation 17 and 18 shows that there is but one Babylon in view. That Babylon is a city that will extend its control throughout the world. However, the city itself still needs to be identified. Chapters 17 and 18 provide little insight by themselves into the identity of the city, but through a comparison with other passages, a positive identification is possible.

The key to identifying the Babylon of Revelation 17 and 18 is to isolate and interpret the Old Testament themes John was drawing on in these chapters. One central Old Testament passage on which Revelation 17 and 18 is constructed is Jeremiah 50 and 51. This is the passage to which John alluded most frequently.

John's use of Jeremiah 50 and 51 can be observed by listing the many parallels between the passages. These parallels fall into three categories: the description, the destruction and the response. Each category will be presented in chart form. Following each chart there will be a brief analysis of the significance of those parallels.

The Description

	JEREMIAH	REVELATION
COMPARED TO A GOLDEN CUP	Babylon has been a golden cup in the hand of the LORD. (Jer. 51:7a)	The woman ... having in her hand a gold cup. (Rev. 17:4; cf. 18:6)
DWELLING ON MANY WATERS	O you who dwell by many waters. (Jer. 51:13)	Then one of the seven angels who had the seven bowls came and spoke with me, saying, "Come here, I will show you the judgment of the great harlot who sits on many waters." (Rev. 17:1)
INVOLVED WITH NATIONS	The nations have drunk of her wine; Therefore the nations are going mad. (Jer. 51:7b)	And those who dwell on the earth were made drunk with the wine of her immorality. (Rev. 17:2b)
NAMED THE SAME	The word which the LORD spoke concerning Babylon, the land of the Chaldeans, through Jeremiah the prophet. (Jer. 50:1)	BABYLON THE GREAT. (Rev. 17:5) Woe, woe, the great city, Babylon, the strong city! For in one hour your judgment has come. (Rev. 18:10)

The Babylon of Jeremiah 50 and 51 and the Babylon of Revelation 17 and 18 are described similarly. Both are described in terms of a golden cup that influences the nations that partake of its contents. Both are also said to dwell on "many waters." Obviously John was employing the terminology used by Jeremiah. Jeremiah was prophesying the destruction of the literal city of Babylon, and John was prophesying the destruction of a city with the same name.

The Destruction

	JEREMIAH	REVELATION
DESTROYED SUDDENLY	Suddenly Babylon has fallen and been broken. (Jer. 51:8)	Standing at a distance because of the fear of her torment, saying, "Woe, woe, the great city, Babylon, the strong city! For in one hour your judgment has come." (Rev. 18:10)
DESTROYED BY FIRE	Their dwelling places are set on fire. (Jer. 51:30)	And the ten horns which you saw, and the beast . . . will eat her flesh and will burn her up with fire. . . . She will be burned up with fire. (Rev. 17:16; 18:8)
NEVER TO BE INHABITED	And it will never again be inhabited. (Jer. 50:39)	So will Babylon, the great city, be thrown down with violence, and will not be found any longer. (Rev. 18:21)
PUNISHED ACCORDING TO DEEDS	Repay her according to her work; According to all that she has done, *so* do to her. (Jer. 50:29)	Pay her back even as she has paid, and give back *to her* double according to her deeds; in the cup which she has mixed, mix twice as much for her. (Rev. 18:6)
FALL ILLUSTRATED	And as soon as you finish reading this scroll, you will tie a stone to it and throw it into the middle of the Euphrates, and say, "Just so shall Babylon sink down and not rise again because of the calamity that I am going to bring upon her; and they will become exhausted." (Jer. 51:63-64)	Then a strong angel took up a stone like a great millstone and threw it into the sea, saying, "So will Babylon, the great city, be thrown down with violence, and will not be found any longer." (Rev. 18:21)

John and Jeremiah each described a city that is destroyed suddenly and completely. A city in full blossom is plucked up never to reappear. The destruction is meted out by God for past deeds and is pictured as a rock sinking in a body of water to rise no more.

The Response

	JEREMIAH	REVELATION
GOD'S PEOPLE TO FLEE	Flee from the midst of Babylon, And each of you save his life! (Jer. 51:6) Come forth from her midst, My people, And each of you save yourselves From the fierce anger of the LORD. (Jer. 51:45)	I heard another voice from heaven, saying, "Come out of her, my people, so that you will not participate in her sins and receive of her plagues." (Rev. 18:4)
HEAVEN TO REJOICE	"Then heaven and earth and all that is in them Will shout for joy over Babylon, For the destroyers will come to her from the north," Declares the LORD. (Jer. 51:48)	Rejoice over her, O heaven, and you saints and apostles and prophets, because God has pronounced judgment for you against her. (Rev. 18:20)

Jeremiah and John recorded the same response to the destruction of their city. Those on earth are warned to flee from the destruction that has now been promised. In heaven there is a call to rejoice, for the destruction signals God's victory over a godless city.

The ultimate identity of Babylon in Revelation 17 and 18 depends on John's use of Jeremiah's prophecy. Was John describing the same event or simply using *Biblical language* to describe a different event? It was shown earlier that Jeremiah 50 and 51 describes a still-future destruction of the literal city of Babylon. Jeremiah directed his prophecy against "Babylon, the land of the Chaldeans" (50:1). As noted earlier, several key elements of Jeremiah's prophecy have never been fulfilled literally. John predicted the destruction of a city with the same name as the city in Jeremiah's prophecy, having the same physical characteristics as the city in Jeremiah's prophecy and destroyed in the same manner as the city in Jeremiah's prophecy.

In addition to Jeremiah 50 and 51, John also seems to be borrowing imagery from Zechariah 5:5-11. Zechariah saw wickedness personified as a woman. John views a woman "having in her hand a gold cup full of abominations and of the unclean things of her immorality" (Rev. 17:4). Zechariah predicted that wickedness would one day dwell again in Shinar, and John identifies a city named "BABYLON THE GREAT" that he describes as "THE MOTHER OF HARLOTS AND OF THE ABOMINATIONS OF THE EARTH" (Rev. 17:5). Zechariah's vision implies that God will someday allow wickedness to become reestablished in Babylon. John pictures Babylon back in existence and describes the woman as the source of all wickedness that has occurred upon the earth.

These parallels lead to the conclusion that John, Jeremiah and Zechariah are pointing to the future destruction of the same city. John so identified his prophecy with the unfulfilled prophecies of Jeremiah that the association is unmistakable. Therefore, the identity of the Babylon in Revelation 17 and 18 is the future rebuilt city of Babylon on the Euphrates River in present-day Iraq. Babylon will once again be restored and will achieve a place of worldwide influence only to be destroyed by the Antichrist in his thirst for power.

Conclusion

It is this author's belief that the Old Testament and New Testament prophecies of Babylon, when interpreted literally, have never been fulfilled. There has never been a time historically when Babylon has been totally desolate and devoid of human habitation. Babylon's fall is said to coincide with God's restoration of His people and their entering into an everlasting covenant with Him.

Perhaps Babylon can serve as a lesson and an encouragement to dispensationalists. Prophecies that appeared incapable of having a literal fulfillment (whether it be the reestablishment of Israel or the rebuilding of Babylon) make more sense as the time for their fulfillment draws closer.

Of course, literal interpretation is not the exclusive property of dispensationalists. Most conservatives would agree with what has just been said. What, then, is the difference between the dispensationalists' use of this hermeneutical principle and the nondispensationalists' use of it? The difference lies in the fact that the dispensationalist claims to use the normal principle of interpretation *consistently* in *all* his or her study of the Bible.[89]

Those who hold to a pretribulational rapture and a dispensational theology would do well to continue to stress the literal interpretation of prophecy—while reexamining their own interpretations to make sure they are being consistent themselves. The literal method of interpretation must remain the hallmark of dispensationalism. The rebuilding of Babylon is simply another example of how literal interpretation can unlock God's prophetic Word.

---

89   Charles Caldwell Ryrie, *Dispensationalism Today* (Chicago: Moody Press, 1965), p. 89.

Future

BABYLON

Study Guide

Why Does Babylon Matter Today?

Introduction

I know what you are thinking: Babylon was not exactly a good place in the Bible, so why in the world would we want it rebuilt? What purpose would a new Babylon serve? Is not Babylon associated with evil in the end times? Or maybe those strange Old Testament prophecies about the fall of Babylon already came true, so what does it matter now?

The Biblical argument for the rebuilding of Babylon matters for three reasons:

1. Interpreting the prophecies of the fall of Babylon requires the strict application of a historical, grammatical and literal interpretation of the Bible, proving that such an approach is effective for interpreting the whole of Scripture.

In other words, the Bible says what it means and means what it says. A serious student of the Bible ought not to interpret some sections literally and others more metaphorically. Such a mixed method leads to inconsistent interpretations and credibility-straining Biblical gymnastics in order to make one part of the Bible match another. For instance, many well-intentioned believers interpret straightforward historical narratives differently than they do prophetic passages. This is like changing your interpretive lenses out between reading Genesis and Revelation.

While literally interpreting the entire Bible matters, it may matter most with regard to prophetic passages. When believers disagree on end times theology, the fracture point can often be traced to a difference in interpretation. In other words, a pretribulational believer is likely a literalist; a posttribulational believer likely is not.

When students of the Bible engage in solid, literal interpretative work, they will witness the rewards of their efforts pay off again and again with the firm insights such an interpretation provides. But to do so requires knowledge of the original historical context of when a particular book of the Bible was written.

To that end, the undergirding arguments of this book heavily rely on historical data, which means knowing who ruled when and what happened during specific years. Such knowledge will help clarify and amplify what the authors of the Bible were trying to tell both their own contemporaries and us today.

2. If the prophecies about the fall of Babylon have yet to come true, their fulfillment still awaits us.

A major opposing voice to the belief that Babylon will and should be rebuilt stems from the errant belief that the prophecies concerning the ancient city's fall have already come true. Much of this study concerns itself with the many Biblically-backed reasons why these prophecies have yet to be fulfilled.

3. The fall of Babylon precedes the second coming of Jesus Christ.

As the end days draw nearer with every new advance in technology and, seemingly, every new conflict in the Middle East, we must be aware of that region's history as well as what the Bible says will one day occur there. When the striking visuals of Revelation become the reality of our TV screens, we need to be the ones who might "(endure) to the end" (Matt. 24:13). The fall of Babylon is but one of many prophecies that must come true before Jesus' triumphant return.

Discussion

What do you know about Babylon?

- "Nothing."

- "It's a bad place."

- "I just know it's in Revelation."

- "It's important, but I'm not sure why."

Where does the name Babylon come from and what does it mean?

- The first Biblical appearance of the root word for Babylon is Genesis 11:9: "Therefore is the name of it called *Babel*; because the LORD did there confound the language of all the earth: and from thence did the LORD scatter them abroad upon the face of all the earth" (KJV, emphasis added).

- *Babel* means "confusion."

- Trivia: Our modern-day word "babble" is popularly thought to have been derived from *babel*.

Where was Babylon located, and where is it located today?

The ancient and present-day locations of Babylon are the same: on a fertile plain between the Tigris and Euphrates, two rivers you may recall as being essential to the dawn of humanity. However, one of Babylon's bounding rivers (the Euphrates) now covers part of its ancient site.

Today, the scant remains of Babylon can be found about 53 miles south of Baghdad, Iraq. Babylon is almost at the beating-heart center of Iraq.

Who were the Babylonians?

No one people group were the Babylonians. Rather, it is better expressed that the people who came across Babylon, fought for it and settled it were the Babylonians-in-residence—until another group came along and did the same.

The earliest Babylonians were of Akkadian descent until the Amorites, an oft-mentioned and powerful people group in the Old Testament, took control of the city in 1894 B.C. and grew a dynasty. After the well-known Amorite leader Hammurabi died, Babylon subsequently fell under Assyrian, Kassite and Elamite rule. Following that Neo-Babylonian Empire (609–539 B.C.), the once grand city was ruled by the Achaemenid, Seleucid, Parthian, Roman and Sassanid empires. In time, Babylon would ultimately become part of the Persian Empire and be dominated by Islam.

Why does it matter that Christians today know anything about Babylon?

Biblical prophecies reveal that Babylon will be rebuilt before the second coming of Jesus Christ. In 1983, Saddam Hussein began rebuilding Babylon, but he had to put his plans on hold in 1990 as the Gulf War began.

We must learn how to correctly interpret the signs of the times, and the continued rehabilitation of the ancient site of Babylon may prove to be one of the more apparent signs we will be given regarding the last days.

Conclusion

The structure of this study asks three major questions:

1. Why do Protestants interpret Babylon spiritually?

2. What happened to Babylon historically?

3. What does the Bible say about Babylon?

This study will thoroughly answer each question, often by first considering its traditional answer and contrasting that to what is found within the Bible through a literal interpretation. Such substantive Biblical evidence ought to remove all doubt from the mind of any serious student of the Bible who can take the words of the Bible at face value.

Further Reading: Genesis 11:1–9.

Spiritual vs. Literal Bible Interpretation

Introduction

To clearly understand why Protestants still tend to spiritualize their interpretation of what *Babylon* means, we must understand the difference between an allegorical interpretation and a literal interpretation of the Bible. Such interpretative means are the subtle difference between, "What does this verse say to you?" versus "What does this verse say?"

For example, athletes the world over have misused Philippians 4:13 time and again: "I can do all things through Christ which strengtheneth me" (KJV). In celebration of a hard-fought victory, they haphazardly apply a positive connotation to a verse whose context is, at best, middling. The Apostle Paul speaks of both abundance and suffering. Within the context of his letter to the Philippians, the verse effectively says, "Regardless of what is happening around me, whether good or ill, Christ has my back." But all too often Christians and non-Christians alike take the verse out of context and apply an allegorical, me-first meaning to it: *I can do all things through Christ who strengthened me just enough to win.*

To interpret spiritually *before* interpreting contextually will lead you to theological ruin. You cannot know what the Bible will say to you until you know what the Bible says.

We will get to what the Bible specifically says about Babylon in the next section. For now, let us discuss why most Christians are prone to interpreting Babylon as almost anything else other than an actual, physical place that will one day be restored.

The historical answer is that Augustine's first major work, *City of God*, released in the early fifth century, made allegorical interpretations of the Bible famous. His book depicted history as an epic fight between the *City of Man* and the *City of God*. These sorts of spiritual interpretations of the Bible proliferated within the Roman Catholic Church until the famous church Reformers Martin Luther and John Calvin came along.

They believed the harlot of Babylon as depicted in Revelation 17 was Rome, and specifically the Catholic Church as led by the Antichrist, the Pope. Though they had previously broken historical ranks in terms of forgoing most allegorical interpretations of the Bible, they simply could not get past what they viewed to be highly coincidental similarities between Old Testament prophecies regarding Babylon and their current-day struggles against the Catholic Church. After all, they were *the* major Reformers, and to categorize Babylon as an evil empire bent on destroying the people of God seemed to be a tailor-made prophecy for their work against the Catholic Church.

Ironically, these Reformers adopted a literal interpretation of the Old Testament prophecies about Babylon while using a spiritual approach to interpret its New Testament prophecies. Both Luther and Calvin believed all of the Old Testament prophecies were fulfilled when Babylon fell to Cyrus in 539 B.C. Most Protestants since then have followed suit. Our next section will prove otherwise, showing why Babylon's prophesied fall has yet to occur.

In fact, it was Luther's and Calvin's staunch refusal to spiritually interpret the Bible that landed them on the Reformation foundation of justification by faith. But even they could not fully get away from at least some allegorical interpretation. To them, contextual interpretation was essential for teaching, but some allegorical interpretation was still useful for illustrating and inspiring.

These Reformers also had to employ allegorical interpretations when literal interpretations seemingly broke down, as was apparently the case in both Luther's and Calvin's assessment of Babylon as the Catholic Church. In the following section, you will discover why this interpretation was incorrect, but the fact remains that even some of the staunchest literalists ever were sometimes prone to falling back onto spiritual interpretations to fit their own preconceived notions of what they wanted the Bible to say—to them.

Discussion

How would you describe the difference between an allegorical interpretation of the Bible and a literal interpretation?

An allegorical interpretation often places self before God, feelings before understanding, and convenience before hard work. A literal interpretation reverses all of that.

Share a time when your understanding of a verse or Bible story changed because of a shift from an allegorical interpretation to a literal interpretation.

Why do you think Christians are prone to *spiritualizing* what we read in the Bible?

It is often a faster way to feel like you have received something beneficial from God through your Bible study. *I do not have enough time to do such intensive study.* We are intrinsically selfish people and cannot help but to look at the Bible and think, *What is in this for me?*

What are some ways that a person can become stronger in being able to interpret the Bible literally?

Here are some examples of things that will strengthen you: Bible study, historical studies, studies like the one you are currently doing, listening to proper sermons, asking for help when you are not sure if you have the correct interpretation.

Conclusion

Now that we have a better understanding of the difference between interpreting the Bible allegorically versus literally and why Protestants still tend to spiritualize *Babylon*, let's get literal: what actually happened to Babylon?

What Actually Happened to Babylon?

A Short History of the City of Babylon

Introduction

To fully understand the Bible's prophecies about Babylon, we must know the city's history. As was fairly typical in the ancient Middle East—and even in the Middle East of the present day—the city was susceptible to turmoil, revolution and the constant threat of being decimated or taken over. Pay particular attention to the time periods of these rulers and how the city of Babylon is described during their reigns, as this is essential information for understanding the Bible's prophecies about Babylon.

689 B.C.: Sennacherib, the king of Assyria, razes Babylon to the ground. For years prior to that devastation, Sennacherib waged war with Merodach-Baladan, the Chaldean king of Babylon. Per the *International Standard Bible Encyclopedia*, Merodach-Baladan had previously "sent an embassy to Hezekiah, king of Judah, apparently shortly after the latter's illness, in order to congratulate him on his recovery of health, and to make with him an offensive and defensive alliance."[1] In other words, Merodach-Baladan may have feared that he would lose control of Babylon without another king's help.

In hearing that a king of Babylon had met with Hezekiah, the prophet Isaiah minced no words when he approached his king: "Behold, the days come, that all that is in thine house, and that which thy fathers have laid up in store until this day, shall be carried to Babylon: nothing shall be left, saith the LORD. And of thy sons that shall issue from thee, which thou shalt beget, shall they take away; and they shall be eunuchs in the palace of the king of Babylon" (Isa. 39:6–7, KJV).

Sennacherib obliterated Babylon, recording in *The Annals of Sennacherib* that he "completely blotted it out." The tablets that comprised the Babylonian Chronicles report that Babylon remained kingless—and likely still desolate—for the next eight years.

681 B.C.: Sennacherib's son, Esarhaddon, begins rebuilding Babylon.

669 B.C: Esarhaddon dies the same year the rebuilding of Babylon

---

1 *International Standard Bible Encyclopedia*, s.v., "Merodach-Baladan," by R. Dick Wilson, <http://biblehub.com/topical/m/merodach-baladan.htm>; Internet; accessed 8 November 2016.

and the restoration of its temples is complete. The project required 12 years.

626 B.C.: Nabopolassar, a former Assyrian official, rises to power in the wake of political turmoil following the death of the Assyrian king Ashurbanipal. Nabopolassar ruled from Babylon. He is considered the father of the Neo-Babylonian Empire as he united many people, including the Medes.

605 B.C.: Nebuchadnezzar, Nabopolassar's son, begins his reign as king of Babylon. He extended his father's power around Babylon's surrounding areas, including orchestrating the destruction of Judah.

562 B.C.: Nebuchadnezzar dies, ending his 43-year reign. The Neo-Babylonian Empire slowly demised as its four subsequent kings (and a coregent) failed to expand, protect or even control the sprawling empire for the next 23 years.

539 B.C.: Cyrus the Great, the Persian leader and founder of the Achaemenid Empire, conquers Babylon. His empire eventually covered most of the Near East, Southwest Asia, Central Asia and the Caucasus. By the time he was done, Cyrus owned the largest known empire in the world up to that time. Per his own words, Cyrus treated both the gods and the inhabitants of Babylon with respect.

522 B.C.: Cambyses II, Cyrus's son and emperor of the Achaemenid Empire, dies. That same year, two revolts in Babylon led Cyrus' second successor, Darius I, to destroy the walls and gates of Babylon—and kill 3,000 of its men—as a show of force.

465 B.C.: Xerxes I, who is most likely the Persian king named Ahasuerus in the book of Esther, destroys Babylon.

450 B.C.: Herodotus, the ancient historian who had described Darius' destruction of Babylon, visits Babylon. Seventy years after the attack, Herodotus described Babylon as a place missing gates but still containing walls. Even its temple for the Babylonian god Marduk and the Tower of Babel still remained upright. If Herodotus' eyewitness account can be believed, the earlier accounts of the full destruction of Babylon are without merit.

331 B.C.: Alexander the Great marches on Babylon, causing its Persian king, Darius III, to flee the city. Darius was swiftly murdered, thus marking the official end of the Achaemenid Empire. Alexander assumed control of Babylon, but still ventured to other lands to continue his conquests.

323 B.C.: Alexander the Great dies in Babylon in the palace of Nebuchadnezzar II. He had spent his waning years attempting to rebuild Babylon to its former glory, including the reconstruction of the Tower of Babel and the new construction of a harbor and a theater. However, his work to rebuild was never finished due to his death.

312 B.C.: Seleucus I seizes Babylon, but establishes the capital city of the bourgeoning Seleucid Empire in Seleucia, just north of Babylon on the Tigris. Despite Babylon becoming a less important city in this time period, both Seleucus and his son, Antiochus I, are known as "King of Babylon."

166–122 B.C.: The Parthians, from ancient Iran and Iraq, overtake the Seleucids. They maintained Babylon as a place of religious importance.

7 B.C.–18 A.D.: In his Geography, whose publish date is unknown, early first-century Greek historian Strabo calls Babylon "a great desert." However, he also described its buildings and its inhabitants.

64–68 A.D.: The Apostle Peter refers to Jewish converts "in Babylon" in 1 Peter 5:13. In other words, that reference to Babylon very likely is not a veiled reference to Rome. Some believe that that verse shows Peter wrote the letter while in Babylon.

94 A.D.: First-century historian Josephus reports that "great numbers" of Jews live in Babylon.

116 A.D.: According to Roman historian Cassius Dio, the Roman emperor Trajan visits Babylon and finds "nothing but mounds and stones and ruins." However, Dio's account may be exaggerated based on further details he provided regarding Trajan's visit.

1165–1173 A.D.: Spanish Jewish historian and traveler Benjamin of Tudela wanders through 300 medieval towns and records his visit to all of them, including Babylon, in *The Travels of Benjamin*. He described it as a still desolate place, though "twenty thousand Jews live within about twenty miles from this place, and perform their worship in the synagogue of Daniel." He also described the palace of Nebuchadnezzar.

1574 A.D.: Leonhard Rauwolf, a German traveler, physician and botanist, records his visit to Babylon as a place that is "demolished and uninhabited," effectively setting the precedent that would take hold for the next half-century about the ruined city of Babylon. However, it is likely that Rauwolf misidentified Al Fallujah, a city 75 miles north, as Babylon.

1899–1917 A.D.: German archaeologist Robert Koldewey excavates the ancient site of Babylon, discovering the Tower of Babel and the Hanging Gardens of Babylon, a present of Nebuchadnezzar I to his wife. In *The Excavations at Babylon*, he reported that he headquartered his excavation from the city of Babylon and that they had found evidence of habitation going back at least a century.

The Recent History of Babylon

1978 A.D.: In personal correspondence to the author of this book, L. Glynne Dairos, assistant secretary of the British School of Archaeology in Iraq, writes of the existence of three modern settlements in Babylon and the government's already executed plan to restore Babylon.

1980–1988 A.D.: Following the Iranian Revolution of 1979, the Iran–Iraq War erupts, which is both a border dispute and a Middle East power grab. To bolster his people's national pride and enflame their centuries-long feud with the Persians of Iran, Iraqi president Saddam Hussein used the rebuilding of Babylon as a symbol of Iraqi nationalism.

September 22, 1987 A.D.: The first Babylon Festival is held, seven years to the day from Iraq's invasion of Iran. The author of this book attended that festival and revealed how much emphasis Saddam Hussein placed on being associated with one of Babylon's most well-known kings, Nebuchadnezzar I. At the festival, Iraq's Minister of Information proclaimed how the Persians had laid siege to Babylon more than two millennia ago and how Iraq's current efforts to rebuild it were a symbol of their present superiority.

1987-1988 A.D.: The author visits Babylon again, confirming that much of it was, in fact, being rebuilt under Saddam Hussein's guidance and political desires.

1990 A.D.: Led by the United States, and in conjunction with 34 other nations, the Gulf War begins against Iraq in response to Iraq invading Kuwait. The rebuilding of Babylon stalls, but it is not harmed in Operation Desert Storm's bombing runs because it was placed on an off-limits list of historical and/or archaeological locations of significance.

The yearly Babylon Festival is suspended. Surprisingly, Saddam Hussein lives through the war.

1991 A.D.: Following the end of the Iraq War, *The New York Times* reports on Saddam's renewed efforts to rebuild Babylon but notes that: "Power and water have been cut off by the allied bombing, and its shops, museums and restaurants are closed."[2]

1992 A.D.: The annual Babylon Festival is reinstated.

Discussion

Why does the history of Babylon matter?

To prove whether Biblical prophecies concerning Babylon have already been fulfilled or not.

What common thread runs through the history of Babylon covered in this section?

Although the city was often described as desolate or in ruins, it was never uninhabited or completely laid to waste. In all of Babylon's ups and downs as a city of cultural importance, it always seemed to revive itself in time.

What story within the history of Babylon do you find most fascinating? Why?

How is Babylon described today?

- "People probably don't even know that Babylon still exists."

- "Probably just like it was back then: desolate."

2 Paul Lewis, "Dollars Can Still Get You Scotch and Waterford Crystal in Baghdad," *New York Times*, May 12, 1991, p. 10.

• "I think most people just associate the word with evil."

Were you aware that Saddam Hussein began rebuilding Babylon? How does that make you feel?

Why is the rebuilding of Babylon important?

Some students may not have an answer for this question, but the leader can point to the next sessions as to what the Bible says about the reconstruction of Babylon. Essentially, the actual, physical rebuilding of Babylon is a prophecy that has yet to come true. When the city is rebuilt in the future, it will be an indelible precursor to the second coming of Christ.

Conclusion

By covering the highlights (and lowlights) of 2,681 years of Babylonian history, it is easy to see that the city has endured much. The history of Babylon is filled with ruler after ruler, often from different empires, seeking to conquer as much territory as possible, taking over the city, only to be conquered themselves in due time. However, despite its tumultuous history and its rise and fall in population and cultural significance, the ancient city of Babylon was never fully wiped away from the Earth as Biblical prophecies have declared it one day will be. Despite it often being cast as a deserted wasteland, the city of Babylon has yet to die, and this is an essential fact for understanding the literal meaning of the Bible's prophecies about the undying city.

Have the Bible's Prophecies about Babylon Come True?

Introduction

Aside from its association with the construction of the Tower of Babel in Genesis 11, the city of Babylon is mentioned at length in four particular books of the Bible: Isaiah 13–23; Jeremiah 50–51; Zechariah 5:5–11; and Revelation 17–18. This session will consider each of these Biblical portions in light of whether or not their respective prophecies have already come true or still remain to be fulfilled.

Before proceeding with each section below, recommend that the students read those chapters prior to discussion.

Isaiah 13–23

By the time Isaiah began his prophetic ministry in the eighth century
B.C., the kingdom of Israel had been split into the Northern Kingdom
(Israel) and the Southern Kingdom (Judah). In fact, when Isaiah began
prophesying, Israel was already under Assyrian captivity in 722 B.C.
Consequently, for possibly as long as 64 years, Isaiah most often proph-
esied against the people of Judah.

However, in chapters 13 and 14 of the book of Isaiah, he turned his
words of rebuke toward the Gentiles, a.k.a. anyone who was not Jewish. In
the long list of cities Isaiah prophesies against, it is notable that Babylon
is the first city mentioned, the city given the most words and the only city
featured in two separate passages.

Some scholars believe these passages about Babylon actually refer to
Assyria for three reasons:

- The text's lack of consistent structuring when introducing a
  new city, particularly the failure to use the word "oracle" when
  referring to Assyria.

- The importance and power of Assyria over Babylon at that
  particular point in time.

- Kings of Assyria also crowned themselves with the title "King
  of Babylon."

But these arguments are easily refuted:

- On multiple occasions, Isaiah 13–23 fails to use the word "oracle"
  to introduce a new city, e.g., Isa. 18:1. Isaiah makes no segue from
  talking about Damascus to talking about Cush, and there is no
  way that the author would have conflated those cities.

- Assuming the author meant Assyria when he wrote Babylon limits
  God's ability to speak to future events. In other words, though

Babylon did not have the cultural importance it once had, it always held theological importance, especially with regard to Isaiah's prediction in Isaiah 39 that Babylon would be the cause of Judah's fall and not Assyria, the menacing powerhouse of Isaiah's day.

- Not all kings of Assyria took on the title "King of Babylon." If they did, it was often for a short period and not automatically taken. Though Sennacherib amassed laudatory titles at an impressive rate, he never crowned himself "King of Babylon" as far as historical inscriptions reveal.

The Fall of Babylon: Isaiah 13:1–14:23

To deduce whether a prophecy has been fulfilled, we must consider its specifics. To that end, let us look at three keys Isaiah presents in his prophecy about the fall of the city of Babylon: its timing, its nature and the results of its destruction.

The Timing of the Destruction

When will the fall of Babylon occur? On "the day of the LORD" (Isa. 13:6). Of course, that is a nebulous answer, but the phrase still reveals an actual answer. A few verses later (13:9), Isaiah describes the day of the Lord, and that description echoes Joel 3:14b–15, written by a possible contemporary of Isaiah.

To be blunt, the day of the Lord is not a day you want to experience. It is the day when God will pour out His stored-up wrath to where the world is made "a desolation" (Isa. 13:9) and neither the sun nor moon will shine. Isaiah 13:12–13 continues the terrible description of the day of the Lord, noting that His wrath will shake "the earth . . . from its place," alluding to the supernatural signs and earthquakes that other prophecies in the Bible describe about the day of the Lord.

The Nature of the Destruction

According to Isaiah 13:14–18, Babylon's destruction will be total. The people of the city will be annihilated, from the strongest of soldiers to the most innocent of children. We know that this part of the prophecy has yet to be fulfilled by way of the history lesson from our last session. Babylon has yet to be completely wiped from the face of the earth.

What is more telling with regard to whether or not this prophecy has already happened is by whose hand such annihilation will come. Isaiah names the group in 13:17: "Behold, I will stir up the *Medes* against them, which shall not regard silver; and as for gold, they shall not delight in it" (KJV, emphasis added).

Many interpreters read this prophecy as having been fulfilled when Cyrus, leader of the Medo-Persian Empire, captured Babylon in 539 B.C. But multiple historical records reveal something fascinating about the Medes: If they were supposed to have annihilated the Babylonians, they did an incredibly poor job. Cyrus' own account and the *Babylonian Record* both reveal that the fall of Babylon in 539 B.C. occurred without bloodshed. Cyrus even wrote, "I strove for peace in Babylon."[3]

Consequently, it makes no sense to say that the Medo-Persian capture of Babylon literally fulfills Isaiah's prophecy when that historical event failed to fulfill *every* detail Isaiah recorded.

The Results of the Destruction

According to Isaiah 13:19–14:2, the total destruction of Babylon will have two specific results:

1. Its destruction will be permanent.

2. Its destruction will serve as a precursor to God's restoration of the nation of Israel.

---

3 Pritchard, *Ancient Near Eastern Texts Relating to the Old Testament*, p. 316.

The permanence of the destruction is seen in Isaiah 13:19–20. The prophet compares the destruction to what happened to Sodom and Gomorrah, but also goes to great lengths to show how utterly permanent Babylon's destruction will be. Once the city has been obliterated, it will not be able to tolerate long-term, short-term or *any*-term habitation. In just one verse (Isa. 13:20), the prophet notes that:

- No one will live there "from generation to generation" (long-term),
- "Nor will the Arab pitch *his* tent there" (short-term),
- "Nor will shepherds make *their flocks* lie down there" (any-term).

Babylon will not even be suitable for a one-night stay by itinerant shepherds.

Very quickly after those verses, Isaiah writes that "the LORD will have compassion on Jacob and again choose Israel, and settle them in their own land" (Isa. 14:1). After the total destruction of Babylon, God will restore His people. In fact, He will restore them to cultural dominance as evidenced by Isaiah 14:2b: "They will take their captors captive and will rule over their oppressors." Again, the details of these prophecies further prove that the fall of Babylon to Cyrus in 539 B.C. did *not* fulfill them. The recorded history of Israel in Ezra, Nehemiah, Haggai and Zechariah do *not show* a dominant Israel following Cyrus' peaceful overtaking of Babylon.

Many consider the prophecy in Isaiah to have been fulfilled in the Persian conquering of Babylon because the facts support the broad strokes of the prophecy: Babylon fell to the Medes and some Israelites returned to their homeland. But the supposed fulfillment of that prophecy falls apart when considering the details: Post-capture, Babylon still flourished, its inhabitants were not killed, the day of the Lord did not arrive, and Israel did not make captives of her captors.

Either Isaiah's prophecies are not supposed to be interpreted literally or they have yet to be fulfilled.

Jeremiah 50–51

One hundred years after Isaiah wrote his prophecies, another prophet predicted that Babylon would attack and destroy Jerusalem. Jeremiah's prophecies came true in 586 B.C. At the time, Nebuchadnezzar reigned over Babylon, and the city was at one of its historical zeniths of being the most powerful and significant of cities in the ancient Near East.

A majority of the book of Jeremiah covers God's words spoken through Jeremiah for the specific benefit of Israel and Judah (Jer. 2–45). But the last five chapters are God's words to the nations. Of those 231 verses that speak to nine ancient nations, 110 verses are reserved for Babylon, far more than any other nation. Echoing Isaiah's prophecies, Jeremiah considers both the timing and the results of Jerusalem's future destruction at the hands of the Babylonians.

The Timing of the Destruction

The phrase Jeremiah uses in Jeremiah 50:4 is revealing: "In those days and at that time." He uses that phrase in whole or in part nine times throughout his book. Save for one exception, every mention concerns the end times. He further narrows down the timing by mentioning that Israel and Judah will come together to "seek" God. Remember, Israel and Judah were divided at this point in history, so it would be of great importance should the severed nation come back together.

Eight times throughout the book of Jeremiah, he connects this rejoining of Israel and Judah with future language such as "in those days" or "days are coming" (e.g., Jer. 23:5). (Again, the specifics of this prophecy argue against the interpretation that it was fulfilled after Babylon fell to Cyrus. Israel and Judah did *not* come together after that overtaking.)

Even more fascinating, Jeremiah reports that the coming together of Israel and Judah will be both physical and spiritual: "They will come that they may join themselves to the LORD *in* an everlasting covenant that will not be forgotten" (Jer. 50:5). In other words, a revival's going to break out. In Jeremiah 50:20, the prophet even says that God will pardon His people and "search will be made for the iniquity of Israel, but there will be none; and for the sins of Judah, but they will not be found." Again, the history of Israel and Judah as recorded in Ezra, Nehemiah, Haggai, Zechariah and Malachi reveal a people who are still sinful and two nations that are still not reconnected.

The Results of the Destruction

With multiple verses supporting each instance, Jeremiah makes four specific prophecies about Babylon's ultimate fall:

1. Babylon's population will be killed.

2. Babylon's buildings will be plundered and its fortifications destroyed.

3. The city and country will be uninhabitable.

4. Only those who "flee" the city will be spared (Jer. 51:6).

In other words, these prophecies from Jeremiah echo what Isaiah said: Babylon will be completely wiped from the face of the earth in a bloody takeover that results in a place that will never be inhabited again. As a reminder, Cyrus' takeover of Babylon in 539 B.C. was peaceful and without bloodshed. Jeremiah also repeats Isaiah's prophecy, which was made almost 100 years earlier, that Babylon's fall would be similar to what happened to Sodom and Gomorrah (Jer. 50:39–40).

Another piece of fascinating evidence to show that Babylon's ultimate fall has yet to happen is the fact that Daniel remained in Babylon despite Jeremiah's warnings that the people of Israel needed to "flee" the city before it was taken over (Jer. 51:6; cf. 50:8; 51:45). Per Daniel 9:2, Daniel knew Jeremiah's writings. Per Daniel 5:30, Daniel was still in Babylon when it fell to the Medes. Why would Daniel not have fled the city then? It's either because he did not understand Jeremiah's prophecies, which seems unlikely, or he knew better: Jeremiah's prophecies concerned a time that was still to come.

From all of these facts, the fall of Babylon as prophesied by both Isaiah and Jeremiah has yet to occur.

Zechariah 5:5–11

Following Cyrus's conquering of Babylon in 539 B.C., a remnant of Israelites was allowed to return to Jerusalem just a year later, in 538 B.C. Cyrus even allowed them to begin rebuilding their temple within Jerusalem. But when that work began in 536 B.C., local opposition soon stopped construction. In 520 B.C., God called the prophet Zechariah to encourage His people to keep working on the temple, but the prophet also spoke to events that would precede the first and second comings of Christ.

Zechariah's prophecies concerning Babylon occur toward the end of his eight *night visions* (Zech. 1:8) recorded in the first half of the book of Zechariah. In Zechariah 5:5–11, he writes of a very strange vision that ultimately concerns Babylon. In so many words, Zechariah sees a woman in an open basket, or "ephah," which is a term of measurement but is used here to denote an ephah-sized container. This basket is covered with lead, effectively encasing the woman.

The angel speaking to Zechariah calls this woman "Wickedness" (5:8). Though it is unclear whether this "Wickedness" refers to the Israelites then in Babylon or to the whole world at the time, one issue is clear from that vision: The "Wickedness" is being contained.

Two angels then escort the bagged "Wickedness" away. Zechariah asks where they are taking her, and their response is very specific: "To build it an house in the land of Shinar: and it shall be established, and set there upon her own base" (Zech. 5:11, KJV). "Shinar" is used eight times in the Old Testament in the NASB and seven times in the KJV, and every mention associates the place with Babylon (Gen. 10:10; 11:2; 14:1; 14:9; Isa. 11:11; Dan. 1:2). In other words, the angels told Zechariah they were taking the captive evil back to Babylon and that a new dwelling would be created for it.

Zechariah wrote those words in 520 B.C. The fall of Babylon to Cyrus occurred in 539 B.C., 19 years *before* Zechariah received that prophecy. Consequently, the vision he was given cannot have been related to the fall of Babylon that had already occurred. Rather, it points to a future instance where an abode of evil will be constructed in Babylon.

It is also notable that the angel personifies evil as a woman. The Apostle John does the same when describing Babylon in Revelation 17, which we will look at in detail in our next section.

Lastly, the chiastic structure Zechariah employs in Zechariah 1:7–6:8 gives further credence to Shinar/Babylon as being an essential evil when the end times come. A chiasm is a literary technique often used in the Bible to highlight particular details. The table included in the text for this Zechariah passage helps visualize what a chiasm is. As the table shows, if each particular section is given a letter, the structure is ABCDDCBA. The "A" sections purposefully echo each other, and the middle sections are often the most important (but not always).

In Zechariah's *night vision* concerning Shinar/Babylon, its chiastic structure echoes one of Zechariah's earlier *night visions* about "four horns" and "four craftsmen" (Zech. 1:18–21). This Biblical imagery parallels the four Gentile powers controlling Jerusalem during "the times of the Gentiles" (Lk. 21:24; end times) in Daniel 2 and 7. The final Gentile power in Zechariah could be the same power with "feet partly of iron and partly of clay" in Daniel 2:33 or "the fourth beast" in Daniel 7:23. This association could be made through John's naming the evil woman "BABYLON" in his vision in Revelation 17 (cf. Rev. 17:5). Babylon and the fourth Gentile empire are associated in John's end-time vision, which likely incorporated Zechariah's prophecies.

However, Zechariah's prophecies alone do not reveal Babylon's future, ultimate role in God's will for our Earth. For that, we must look toward the end of Revelation.

Discussion

What four books of the Bible devote major sections to Babylon's ultimate fall?

Isaiah, Jeremiah, Zechariah and Revelation.

In Isaiah 13–23, how can we be assured that the Babylon mentioned in those passages *is not* actually ancient Assyria, as some interpreters would have us believe?

Not all cities were introduced with the word "oracle." Assuming that Isaiah meant Assyria limits God's ability to speak to future events. Lastly, not all kings of Assyria assumed the title "King of Babylon."

What three keys in Isaiah 13–14 offer insight into whether its prophecy of the fall of Babylon has already occurred?

The timing of the destruction of Babylon, the nature of that destruction and the results of that destruction.

How do we know that the Medo-Persian conquering of Babylon in 539 B.C. was not the prophetic fall of Babylon?

The people of Babylon were not annihilated, nor was there bloodshed. Furthermore, Babylon was still inhabited following its conquest by Cyrus and Israel did not make captives of her captors.

What two keys in Jeremiah 50–51 reveal that the fall of Babylon has yet to occur?

The timing of the destruction of Babylon and its results.

In Jeremiah 50:4 and 20, what does "in those days and at that time" mean?

The end times, a time yet to come.

What are the four specific prophecies Jeremiah makes about the result of Babylon's fall?

1. Babylon's population will be killed.
2. Babylon's buildings will be plundered and its fortifications destroyed.
3. The city and country will be uninhabitable.
4. Only those who flee the city will be spared.

What does Zechariah's vision of a woman in a basket being covered by lead mean?

The wickedness of Babylon will be contained for a time.

What is a chiasm, and why is it important to interpreting the prophecies of the fall of Babylon?

A chiasm is a literary structure that mirrors itself (ABCCBA) in order to bring attention to that which is central to the structure and to draw parallels between similar themes. In Zechariah 1, the chiastic structure helps reveal Shinar as another name for Babylon and a place of evil during the end times.

Further Reading: Isaiah 13–23, Jeremiah 50–51 and Zechariah 5:5–11

Do Two Babylons Exist
in Revelation 17–18?

The traditional interpretation of Revelation 17–18 holds that the Babylons described in each chapter are actually separate Babylons: the Babylon in Revelation 17 is ecclesiastical Babylon, which will be destroyed by the Antichrist in the middle of the tribulation, while the Babylon of Revelation 18 is economic Babylon, which is the Antichrist's capital that will be destroyed at the end of the tribulation. So, do both of these Babylons need to fall in order for the Old Testament prophecies to come true? Or do these Revelation depictions of two seemingly separate Babylons actually represent one city that will ultimately be decimated according to the prophecies in Isaiah, Jeremiah and Zechariah?

Arguments Against One Babylon in Revelation 17–18

Interpreters in favor of *two Babylons* point to four major differences between these two chapters: they apparently describe different settings, destroyers, responses and characterization.

Different settings: Two different angels present two different visions to John. The central issue with regard to whether these chapters have different settings is Revelation 18:1: *"And after these things* I saw another angel come down from heaven, having great power; and the earth was lightened with his glory"* (KJV, emphasis added). Does "after these things" refer to the vision of the future John had or to his present time, i.e., the actual time in which he is receiving that vision?

Those who argue for two Babylons assert that "after these things" means the vision of Revelation 18 will take place *after* the vision of Revelation 17 takes place. But where that phrase is used elsewhere in the Bible, such as in the book of John, it simply means a gap in *present* time occurred. The key word to look for is what follows the phrase: "And after these things *I saw.* . . ." In both his gospel and in Revelation, when John follows "after these things" with a verb of perception (saw, heard, etc.), he is referring to his own time and not some future date. In other words, when the vision of Revelation 18 comes true, it does not necessarily follow the vision of Revelation 17 coming true. However, John *received* the vision of Revelation 17 before he received the vision of Revelation 18.

So, the two Babylons could be one and the same.

Different destroyers: *Two Babylon* interpreters also say that Revelation 17 and 18 present two different destroyers—kings (17:16) versus fire (18:8)—and two different reasons for its destruction—man (17:16) versus God (18:8). But a closer inspection of these chapters reveals more similarities than differences. In fact, these chapters actually tell of the same destruction of one Babylon but focus on different aspects of its annihilation.

The arguments against these chapters depicting different destroyers look at particular verses that help us make sense of the seeming inconsistencies. In the same chapter where Babylon is destroyed by kings, Revelation 18:8 says that the city "will be burned up with fire," the same as Revelation 17:16 attests. In the same chapter where Babylon is destroyed by men, Revelation 17:17 says, "God has put it in their hearts to execute His purpose," the same as Revelation 18:8 attests. The chart included in the text provides more examples of these chapters' similarities.

Different responses: The kings of the end times apparently respond differently to Babylon's fall. In Revelation 17:16, the "ten horns" ("ten kings," Rev. 17:12) "hate the harlot" (Babylon) and desire to lay waste to the city. Revelation 18:9 says that "the kings of the earth . . . will weep and lament." Hatred versus weeping is certainly a stark contrast.

If the two chapters are not discussing two Babylons, only one other conclusion can be drawn: The two chapters are discussing two distinct groups of kings. The terminology used to describe these kings helps define that distinction. "The ten horns" (Rev. 17:7, 12, 16) are those rulers who will have united themselves to the beast in order to plot her overthrow. "The kings of the earth" (Rev. 17:2, 18; 18:3, 9; 19:19) are the rest of the rulers in the world who, by then, rely far too heavily on Babylon for their economic well-being. Seen in those lights, it then makes sense that the ten horns would hate Babylon's destruction and the kings of the earth would weep after its fall.

Different characterization: *Two Babylon* interpreters hold that Revelation 17 characterizes Babylon as a religious center and Revelation 18 characterizes the city as a commercial center. This stems from the very different types of visions John receives in each chapter. In Revelation 17, evil is personified as a woman. In Revelation 18, the vision is more direct and personifies evil as a city. Revelation 17:18 ties the two chapters together: "And the woman which thou sawest is that great city, which reigneth over the kings of the earth" (KJV). In other words, the woman is Babylon; Babylon is the woman.

Per this interpretation and the other issues refuted above, it is challenging for this author to agree with the *two Babylons* interpretations. The Babylons of Revelation 17 and 18 are the same city.

Parallels Between Revelation 17 and 18

When inspecting the details of these chapters, similarities begin to leap off of the page, as evidenced by the charts within the main text. In both chapters the city is called "BABYLON THE GREAT" (17:5; cf. 18:2) and described as a "great city" (17:18) or "strong city" (18:10). The woman of chapter 17 and the city of chapter 18 both wear "purple and scarlet . . . adorned with gold" (17:4a; 18:16). And they both hold a "cup" (17:4b; 18:6).

In both chapters, "the kings of the earth committed *acts of* immorality" with her and the nations get "drunk with the wine of her immorality" (17:2; cf. 18:3). She drinks "the blood of the saints" (17:6) and "the blood of prophets" (18:24), symbolizing persecution. Lastly, fire destroys her/the city because God has allowed it to be so (17:16–17; 18:5, 8).

It is very challenging to view these many similarities as describing two different Babylons.

The Larger Context of Revelation 17–18

As if those two chapters did not present enough evidence, the preceding and succeeding chapters provide more proof of a "one Babylon" interpretation. Revelation 14:8 says, "Fallen, fallen is Babylon the great, she who has made all the nations drink of the wine of the passion of her immorality," echoing multiple points of similarity with both chapters 17 and 18. Revelation 16:19 again names the city "Babylon the great" and speaks of "the cup of the wine of His fierce wrath."

In Revelation 19:2, John describes the heavenly chorus rejoicing over Babylon's fall, saying that God "has judged the great harlot who was corrupting the earth with her immorality," again implying that the harlot is Babylon and Babylon is the harlot. The song of praise recorded in Revelation 19:1–5 seems to refer to just one fall of Babylon.

Four Interpretative Keys that Prove Babylon is the Harlot of Revelation 17

Revelation 17:1–18 describes a prostitute astride a scarlet beast. How can we know this is the city of Babylon?

1. Babylon is a harlot.

First, the Old Testament prophets often equated prostitution with idolatry, or man's spiritual infidelity with God. For a prophet to describe a nation as a harlot would be nothing new. However, the reference in Revelation 17 refers more to Babylon prostituting itself for economic, rather than spiritual, gain.

By describing Babylon as a harlot, John was also contrasting the cities of Jerusalem and Babylon. Jerusalem is "the bride, the wife of the Lamb" (Rev. 21:9) while Babylon is "the great harlot who sits on many waters" (Rev. 17:1). Other stark contrasts are also made clear in the chart included in the text.

2. Babylon is a mystery.

In Revelation 17:5, "mystery," or *mysterion* in the Greek, is written upon the harlot's "forehead." Some debate exists as to what that "mystery" actually refers to: Is mystery part of her name, or is her name a mystery?

Because other verses in Revelation (14:8; cf. 16:19; 18:2) call the city "Babylon the great" and not "MYSTERY, BABYLON THE GREAT" (17:5, KJV) the latter interpretation seems more probable: It is a mystery why she is named "Babylon the great."

But how is her name a mystery? Some propose that *mysterion* means her name ought to be interpreted symbolically, but the term denotes the availability of truth rather than the quality of truth. In other words, can this mystery be known? When a similar word, *mysterion*, is used elsewhere in the New Testament, it denotes a truth that has been or is being revealed. The secret can be known. This makes sense in the grander genre of Revelation: *apocalypses* means "revelation," something that has been revealed.

Ultimately, God described the harlot as a mystery to John because it was something that had yet to be fully revealed to man. It was a mystery waiting to be made known. This revelation pulled back the spiritual curtains on what John saw would come true in time. John saw two end-time world powers, the prostitute and the beast she rode in on, existing at the same time. The angel even blatantly tells John, "I will tell you the mystery (*mysterion*) of the woman and of the beast that carries her" (Rev. 17:7).

3. Babylon is a city.

Revelation 17:18 ought to refute any interpretations that the woman is anything other than the actual rebuilt city of Babylon: "The woman whom you saw is the great city, which reigns over the kings of the earth." God identifies her first as a city, not an ecclesiastical system. Remember: the separation of church and state did not exist in John's time. Back then, the city was first and foremost the city itself and likely did not stand in as a representation of the systems it controlled or its religious functions.

4. Babylon sits on seven mountains.

In Revelation 17:9–10, the angel interprets the vision to John. "The seven heads" on the beast that the woman (Babylon) rides represent "seven mountains." In antiquity and in John's day, everyone knew that a seven-hilled city was Rome. But this interpretation has flaws:

- The woman and the beast are not the same entity, and the seven hills are associated with the beast, not the woman. If the seven hills refer to Rome, then it ought to be inferred that the Antichrist's empire will be in Rome, not Babylon. In this instance, the woman's (Babylon) location is not even mentioned.

- The woman's act of sitting on the hills (Rev. 17:9) does not refer to her location, but rather to her power and control. Revelation 17:1 says she "sits on many waters," and 17:15 interprets those "waters" as "peoples and multitudes and nations and tongues." In other words, she rules what she sits upon. Consequently, she controls the beast (and the Antichrist and the kings allied with him) because she sits upon the beast. To consistently interpret Scripture, the harlot's act of sitting must always equate to the harlot's power.

- Revelation is based in Jewish history. Instead of asking how antiquity would have understood a seven-mountain city, we ought to ask how the Old Testament presented a seven-mountain city. "Mountain" was most often used as a symbolic reference to a kingdom or national power. See Isaiah 2:2, Jeremiah 51:25 and Daniel 2:35, 44 for examples.

- The mountains in Revelation 17 are both mountains and kings. First, Rome's history prevents ancient Rome from being the fulfillment of that prophecy. It is difficult, if not impossible, to make the history of Rome's rulers align with the seven kings of the Revelation 17 vision. It would require leaving out at least three valid Roman emperors from such a lineup. Additionally, the way in which the prophet Daniel uses "king" and "kingdom" interchangeably (Daniel 2:37–39), where the king symbolizes his kingdom, is a precursor to the way John uses the same terms in Revelation 17–18.

To review, Babylon is a mysterious harlot of a city sitting on seven hills. Interpreted, this means the literal city of Babylon, drunk on its own power and greed, will dominate the world by controlling the Antichrist and his kingly minions. The four interpretative keys unlock the door to a powerful, actual city—not some mystical system of religion.

The Four Parallels Between Revelation 17–18 and Jeremiah 50–51

Though Revelation 17–18 goes into great detail about the city and its role in the future, it does not explicitly say *where* the city will be located. However, parallels with Jeremiah 50–51, a passage which John alluded to most frequently, offer insight. The charts within the text outline these passages' striking similarities in terms of description, destruction and response.

The descriptions of Babylon in Jeremiah and Revelation both refer to a golden cup, its dwelling place by "many waters" (Rev. 17:1), its drunken involvement with the nations and its naming. Furthermore, as we have already discussed, both chapters refer to Babylon's sudden, total, never-to-be-inhabited-again destruction by fire as punishment for her deeds. In both passages, a stone thrown into water represents Babylon's ultimate fall. Both sections also reveal Earth and heaven's response to Babylon's demise: God's people "flee" (Jer. 51:6) while heaven rejoices over God's victory over a godless city.

John predicted the destruction of a city with the same name, having the same physical characteristics and destroyed in the same manner as the city in Jeremiah's prophecy. Because John so closely adheres to the many descriptions of Babylon's fall in Jeremiah 50–51, and because we have already established that Jeremiah's prophecies have yet to come true, it must hold true that John and Jeremiah spoke about the same Babylon. John also references Zechariah 5:5–11, calling back to "Wickedness" (Zech. 5:8) personified as a woman with a gold cup who will one day reinhabit Shinar. Zechariah's vision implies that God will someday allow "Wickedness" to become reestablished in Babylon, and John's vision confirms Zechariah's prophecy.

Ultimately, the prophecies of John, Jeremiah and Zechariah all point to the future destruction of the same city: Babylon the Great. The identity of the Babylon in Revelation 17–18 is the future rebuilt city of Babylon on the Euphrates River in present-day Iraq. Babylon will once again be restored and will achieve a place of worldwide influence only to be destroyed by the Antichrist in his thirst for power.

Discussion

What is the traditional interpretation of Revelation 17–18 concerning the harlot and the city of Babylon?

That they are two different Babylons: one spiritual in nature and one concrete.

What four reasons do interpreters give for believing that these chapters describe two different Babylons?

Different settings, different destroyers, different responses and different characterization.

How do we know that the Babylons of Revelation 17 and 18 are actually the same Babylon?

Both are named "BABYLON THE GREAT" (Rev. 17:5; cf. 18:2) wield a cup and wear purple and scarlet. Both persecute believers and both are consumed by fire per God's will. Both make the nations "drunk" on "immorality" (Rev. 17:2).

What are the four interpretative keys that prove Babylon is the harlot and the harlot is Babylon?

1. The Old Testament represented unfaithful nations as harlots.

2. The woman and the city are both mysteries in terms of a revelation that has now been revealed.

3. The city is a concrete, actual city—not a spiritual metaphor.

4. Though the city sits on seven hills, it is not representative of Rome.

What is more likely? That the prophecies of Isaiah, Jeremiah, Zechariah and John describe an event that has already happened or an event that is still to come? Explain your reasoning with what you have learned in this session.

Why does any of this matter?

Conclusion

The author firmly believes that the prophecies of the fall of Babylon have yet to occur. Consequently, prophecies that could not have been literally fulfilled near John's day have a greater possibility of coming true as the time of their fulfillment draws closer.

Note that we have arrived at this conclusion by choosing to *consistently* and *literally* interpret all of Scripture. Just because Revelation seems so figurative does not mean its ultimate fulfillment will not be something quite literal. We would do well to remember the lesson of consistent, literal interpretation in all of our Bible reading, from Genesis all the way through Revelation. The rebuilding of Babylon is but one example of how literally interpreting the Bible can unlock what seems hidden just behind the words of the Bible.

Further Reading: Revelation 17–18

Dispensational Publishing House is striving to become the go-to source for Bible-based materials from the dispensational perspective.

Our goal is to provide high-quality doctrinal and worldview resources that make dispensational theology accessible to people at all levels of understanding.

Visit our blog regularly to read informative articles from both known and new writers.

And please let us know how we can better serve you.

Dispensational Publishing House, Inc.
Taos, NM.

DispensationalPublishing.com

CPSIA information can be obtained
at www.ICGtesting.com
Printed in the USA
LVOW10s0013150317
527250LV00029B/700/P